P9-DUJ-181

THE AMNESTY INTERNATIONAL HANDBOOK

Amnesty International campaigns for the release of men and women who are imprisoned for their political or religious beliefs or for their race, color, language, or ethnic origin, provided they have not used or advocated violence. These people are called "Prisoners of Conscience."

Amnesty International opposes torture, inhuman treatment, and the death penalty in all cases and without reservation. It advocates fair and speedy trials for all political prisoners.

Amnesty is financed by its members and supporters throughout the world, by subscription and donation.

Nobel Peace Prize 1977   UN Human Rights Prize 1978

DEDICATION

Dedicated on Amnesty International's 30th Anniversary
to the thousands of men and women still incarcerated
around the world because of their consciously held
beliefs, opinions, religion, sex, or race.

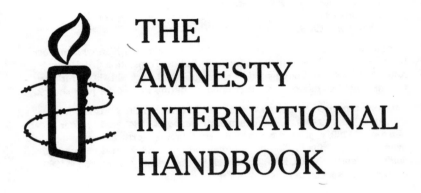

THE
AMNESTY
INTERNATIONAL
HANDBOOK

Compiled and edited by

Marie Staunton, Sally Fenn,
and Amnesty International U.S.A.

Claremont, CA

© 1991 Amnesty International

First US edition published in 1991
by Hunter House Inc., Publishers.

Hunter House Inc., Publishers
P.O. Box 847
Claremont, CA 91711-0847

Quotation on page 36 from *Prisoner Without a Name, Cell Without a Number*
by Jacobo Timerman, translated by Toby Talbot. Translation ©1981 by
Alfred A. Knopf, Inc. Copyrighted as an unpublished work. ©1980 by African
International Productions, NV. Reprinted by permission of the publisher.

Cartoons reprinted by permission of: Jeff Danziger in the *Christian Science
Monitor* ©1989, 1990. J. B. Handelsman in *Playboy* ©1984. Fred Wagner in *NY
Newsday* ©1989, reprinted by special permission of North America
Syndicate, Inc. Dana Fradon in *The New Yorker* ©1983. Mort Gertberg in
Saturday Review ©1969. Mike Luckovich in *The Atlanta Constitution* ©1989,
reprinted by special permission of Creators Syndicate.

Library of Congress Cataloging-in-Publication Data

Amnesty International handbook/edited by Marie Staunton, Sally Fenn.
— 1st U.S. ed.
p.   cm.
Includes index.
ISBN 0-89793-081-9 : $9.95
1. Amnesty International. 2. Human rights. I. Staunton, Marie.
II. Fenn, Sally. III. Amnesty International.
JC571.A45   1991
323' .06'01—dc20   91–12255
                                                                              CIP

Book and cover design by Qalagraphia
Cover illustration "La Colombe et le Prisonnier" by Pablo Picasso, 1959
US edition edited by Marjorie Wilson
Production Manager: Paul Frindt
Publisher: Kiran S. Rana
Set in 10/13 point Cheltenham by 847 Communications, Claremont, CA
Text printed on recycled paper
Printed by Delta Lithograph, Valencia, CA
Manufactured in the United States of America

9 8 7 6 5 4 3 2 1   First edition

CONTENTS

ACKNOWLEDGMENTS

Amnesty International would like to thank all those who contributed to this book, with particular thanks to Ron Lajoie, Jean Freedberg, Nick Rizza, Ellen Moore, Cosette Thompson, Alice Miller, Janice Christensen, Ellen Lutz, Geraldine Van Bueren, Alex Milne, Jenny Stephenson, Jan Shaw, Anne Rimmer, Dan Jones, Ian Pearce, Tony Jones, and Michael Crowley.

Several cartoons carried over from the U.K. edition are taken from *And now for the next sketch . . . Cartoons for Amnesty,* published by Amnesty International in 1986. The following donated additional cartoons, some of them done specifically for this book: Alfieri & Colley, Joan Baez, Jeff Danziger, Dana Fradon, Mort Gertberg, J. B. Handelsman, Mike Luckovich, Henry Martin, Mick Stevens, and Fred Wagner.

PREFACE

"It was more than 15 years ago that I first heard of Amnesty International. It was at a time when some of my closest friends had fallen victim to the secret police. In panic and distress, I searched for someone, somewhere to try and save their lives.

"In view of the fear generated by the repressive regime in my country—Morocco—many did not dare to associate themselves with political activists. It was then, in a moment of desperation, that I came across a little leaflet which spoke about an organization purporting to care about those prisoners who may be 'forgotten.'

"It was Amnesty International. I wrote to them in great haste, asking for help on behalf of my friends. As I did so the thought crossed my mind that someone might do the same for me one day if I should get into the same situation.

"It was not so long afterwards that I was in this dreaded situation. My 'crime' was to dare to speak out against injustice and repression in Morocco. On the night of January 9, 1976, a cold and windy night, a group of armed secret policemen broke into my flat and took me, handcuffed and blindfolded, to a secret location. My daily life then became like the accounts I had read, and like the sort of things my countrymen used to speak of in hushed voices.

"For eight long months, I was held in secret detention where I was permanently handcuffed and blindfolded and periodically tortured. Then one morning, I was taken out into the daylight and transferred to a normal prison in Casablanca. After eight months of darkness, a normal prison was for me like a luxury hotel: to be able to be free of the handcuffs and blindfold, to see the sky—however distorted through the iron bars of the window in my tiny cell—was such a welcome change.

"But my new satisfaction with this change disappeared when I realized that now I was facing the prospect of years of detention without trial. It was only after a hunger strike that I was eventually given a trial—but what a farce of a trial! The outcome was a ten-year prison sentence and two extra years for exposing the torture and protesting about the unfairness of my trial. The judges called my attitude 'a misbehavior in court.'

"Prison conditions were very harsh when I started serving my sentence. They did not improve until, along with other prisoners, I went on a succession of hunger strikes—for three months during the year.

"It was in the darkness of my humid cell that I received my first reassuring sign: a letter from Amnesty International. It was a sign of hope, and the determination of those outside not to let the oppressors crush a voice in the darkness of the inhuman and notorious Kenitra Prison.

"For years some wonderful men and women campaigned for my release. They did not have to share my views to call for my release. They 'adopted' me because they reckoned that I should be entitled to express my beliefs without the fear of torture and a 12-year prison sentence. It was because of their persistent work that my oppressors were unable to place me in the category of forgotten prisoners. The letters were a constant reminder that even people at the other end of the world share human indignation about the oppression of someone who holds differing views from an unelected regime.

"It was the accumulation of a variety of actions undertaken by this brave group of Amnesty members which over the years managed to break the wall of silence my oppressors tried to build around me, and which led to my release.

"During eight years in prison I was able to witness what a vital need there is for an organization such as Amnesty. Without it, I would still have been the forgotten prisoner in the notorious Casablanca secret detention center, instead of enjoying the precious freedom I have today."

Jamal Benomar was imprisoned in 1976 for being a member of an organization opposed to the Government of Morocco. He was adopted by an Amnesty group in Stockholm, who campaigned on his behalf and corresponded with him while he was in prison. Released in November 1983, he is now a researcher at the International Secretariat of Amnesty International in London.

INTRODUCTION

Jamal Benomar's story, told in the Preface, is not unique. Today there are untold thousands of men, women, even children detained in prisons around the world because they dared express ideas considered "offensive" by their government.

Forty years ago the governments of the United Nations proclaimed, for the first time in history, that all human beings would be recognized as free and equal in dignity and rights. That was the promise of the Universal Declaration of Human Rights adopted by the General Assembly in 1948.

That promise has not been kept. Basic rights are denied to millions. People are arrested for their beliefs, tortured, and killed. In many countries even the right to speak up in defense of human rights is being crushed.

This cruelty and injustice must stop. The business of governments is to protect people—the lives and rights not only of their own citizens but also of citizens in other countries.

With more than one million members in 150 countries, Amnesty International is the world's largest organization of its kind helping prisoners like Jamal Benomar. And membership in Amnesty International consists of much more than writing a check once a year.

We are first and foremost an activist organization, a labor intensive organization, that is what makes us unique. Everyone who joins Amnesty International is a valuable participant in the most important struggle of our time, the struggle for human rights. You are invited to play a vital role in this struggle.

There are many ways you can do this. We will examine all of them in this book. The work can be difficult and sometimes frustrating, but you get something immeasurable back. You get the indescribable satisfaction that comes when you learn that someone on whose behalf you have written and worked has been set free, or when you learn that a telegram you sent may have literally saved a human life.

A faded envelope with an exotic stamp may arrive in the mail.

"Dear Friends," Chief Gani Fawehinmi, a Nigerian lawyer arrested in June 1989 because of his opposition to the government, wrote members of AIUSA's Urgent Action Network, "I want to place on record my profound and heartfelt appreciation for all your efforts to free me from the illegal detention of the military government of President Ibrahim Babangida . . . . I will always treasure the memory of your contribution to my freedom."

Membership in Amnesty International is an intensely personal experience.

Life-long friendships have been established over thousands of miles. Former prisoners frequently become close friends of the people who have worked so tirelessly on their behalf.

A group in Asheville, North Carolina had worked on the case of an Argentine family that had "disappeared" in Uruguay for years without any response. One day, just before Christmas, a letter arrived. Thanks to an anonymous tip, the family's 23-month-old child had been located and returned to the child's grandparents in Buenos Aires.

"Hallelujah. Paula is with us, with her family. Isn't it beautiful!" wrote the child's grandmother.

"I know of nothing that I do that gives me as much satisfaction as my membership in Amnesty International," said a member in Rhode Island, "I feel involved and no longer helpless. I feel part of a movement. One that really does make a difference."

"I want to thank you," former Yugoslav prisoner of conscience Momcila Selic told Amnesty International members in Washington, DC, "I am a living example that what you do works."

Members are an extraordinary group of people. They are committed, stubborn, idealistic, realistic. They write letters—thousands of them. Some sponsor concerts and film screenings, others speak before schools and religious groups and spread the word about human rights.

They are medical professionals, high school students, senior citizens, trade unionists, plumbers, the famous and the not so famous. They are writers, secretaries, women's activists, and teachers. They come from all shades of the political spectrum.

But they all share one commitment. A commitment to making this world a better place for all, a place where people are no longer imprisoned solely for their beliefs, where people are not tortured or executed.

They are active participants in perhaps the most important movement in modern history. This book shows how you too can become involved.

Sally Artz

 ISSUES THAT
AMNESTY
INTERNATIONAL
ADDRESSES

Chapter One
ABOUT AMNESTY INTERNATIONAL

When Amnesty International was founded in 1961 it was called "one of the larger lunacies of our time." It seemed absurd that ordinary people could help men, women, and children they had never seen in countries they had never visited by writing polite letters to foreign governments. But it works: Since its inception, Amnesty International has adopted or investigated more than 42,000 prisoner cases and we have been able to close more than 38,000. Today, human rights are firmly established on the international agenda. No longer can governments turn a blind eye when their human rights records are called into question.

More than one million people worldwide, from school children to pensioners of all races and politics, in 150 countries, are now working for Amnesty International's three goals:

— The release of prisoners of conscience.These are people detained for their beliefs, color, sex, ethnic origin, language, or religion who have not used or adovated violence

— Fair and prompt trials for all political prisoners

— An end to the death penalty and torture or other cruel, inhuman, and degrading treatment or punishment of all prisoners without reservation.

These goals are the essence of Amnesty International's mandate and your help is needed to achieve them. As with any struggle, what determines whether the human rights movement advances or retreats is, in the end, the balance of forces.

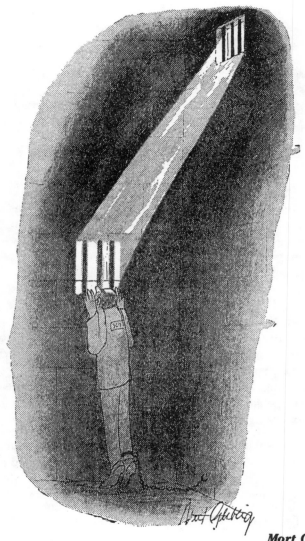

Mort Gertberg

Our forces do not consist of armies or governments, but of men and women who are prepared to commit themselves to the struggle for human rights. When a victim is released from unjust imprisonment or is granted a fair trial, human rights score victories. When torture ceases or executions are prohibited, human rights take a great step forward.

"I feel like a different person, just knowing there is a group that intervenes for human rights," wrote the wife of a political prisoner held in Eastern Europe. "A letter such as one from Amnesty International gives a person strength and makes one feel human again." The prisoner, arrested for criticizing his government in 1981, was freed in April 1987. For six years, two Amnesty International local volunteer groups, one in the Netherlands and one in Canada, had worked for his release. "Mainly I owe my early release to you and your work on my case," he wrote recently to members of the groups.

THE FOUNDING OF AMNESTY INTERNATIONAL

In November 1960, Peter Benenson, a 40-year-old British lawyer, read a newspaper report about two Portuguese students in Lisbon during the Salazar dictatorship. They had been arrested and sentenced to seven years' imprisonment for raising their glasses in public in a toast to freedom.

Incensed by this, Benenson began to consider ways in which the Portuguese authorities—and other oppressive regimes—could be persuaded to release such victims of injustice. His idea was to bombard governments with letters of protest at the imprisonment of prisoners of conscience.

Together with Eric Baker, a prominent English Quaker, Louis Blom-Cooper, a renowned lawyer, and others, he launched a one-year campaign called "Appeal for Amnesty, 1961" to highlight the fate of political prisoners worldwide.

The campaign was launched with an article which appeared in the *London Observer* on May 28, 1961, focusing on eight "forgotten prisoners." The article received a tremendous response: letters of support and money arrived, details of many, many more prisoners were sent, and volunteers eager to work for the release of prisoners of conscience came forward. Amnesty International was born.

A WORLDWIDE CAMPAIGN

Amnesty International is a worldwide campaign for victims of human rights abuse. Its volunteer groups adopt prisoners of conscience, work to end torture and the death penalty throughout the world, and put pressure on governments through letter writing, public demonstration, media outreach, and other techniques.

Amnesty has more than 4,200 local groups around the world. At the end of November 1990, Amnesty International was working on more than 3,000 cases involving more than 4,500 individuals in 83 countries. The good news was that 1,296 cases were closed in the first eleven months of 1990.

Increasingly, Amnesty groups in trade unions, on college and high school campuses, in churches, and among doctors, lawyers, teachers, women, and those working with children, are coordinating their efforts. Using their contacts and their ingenuity, they bring pressure to bear on governments to respect human rights. An increasing number of groups of police officers or ex-military personnel use their experience and persuasive powers to stop their counterparts in other countries abusing human rights.

In this work, Amnesty's mandate to remain independent, impartial, and voluntary is carefully safeguarded, and all members of Amnesty International obey clear rules when working for individuals.

Central to this is financial independence—no money is now accepted from governments. The whole international organization, which employs 250 researchers and has offices in 46 countries, is run entirely on contributions from its members and supporters and hundreds of thousands of donations from around the world. And all the fundraising is the responsibility of the movement's groups and sections—there is no central fundraising program. Each national section solicits its own members, produces and sells its own keyrings and T-shirts, promotes concerts, runs television campaigns, and does whatever else it can to raise money for victims of human rights abuse.

To ensure impartiality, no AI member works on behalf of prisoners held in their own country. However, they can address their own countries' human rights policies. In 1989, for example, during a worldwide campaign to abolish the death penalty, many sections lobbied their own governments to repeal the death penalty. National sections also urged their governments to sign and ratify human rights treaties.

It is essential that Amnesty groups show that they are politically and geographically balanced by campaigning to end patterns of abuse in a range of countries across the geo-political spectrum.

HOW AMNESTY WORKS

The work of Amnesty International is carried out by an army of volunteers, making AI a truly voluntary organization. The first step in any Amnesty campaign is obtaining reliable information. This is done by scanning official sources, sending missions to a country, sending lawyers to observe trials, and by interviewing witnesses. Once the information has been checked and verified, it is released to the public. As word spreads about the human rights violations involved, the pressure on the government builds. Sometimes government authorities respond to AI concerns in private meetings with representatives of Amnesty International; sometimes they respond directly to the volunteers who send them letters.

For example, members of local groups in Hong Kong and Mexico who participated in the campaign against human rights violations in Iran received acknowledgment of their letters from the office of the Iranian Speaker of Parliament. An Iranian provincial public relations official also corresponded with group members in Denmark and the Federal Republic of Germany.

Many state governors and other officials in the United States responded to Amnesty's campaign to end the death penalty here. The Norwegian Section arranged television broadcasts of interviews with governors of states which permit the death penalty. In Mauritius, the campaign received prime-time television coverage. Editorials and news articles published throughout the United States helped to focus debate on the death penalty as a violation of a basic human right.

Human rights activists worldwide use their own creativity to serve human rights campaigns. In Bangladesh, members sponsored a poster exhibition to draw public attention to an adopted prisoner of conscience. In Luxembourg, members invited the public to buy Amnesty International candles and place them in windows to commemorate Human Rights Day, December 10. Thousands of Spanish schools participated in a human rights essay contest organized by Amnesty, and Japanese members held a walkathon for prisoners of conscience worldwide.

The human rights championed by Amnesty International are the same that most governments have already promised to uphold. In 1948, the nations of the world united to proclaim the Universal Declaration of Human Rights in response to the horrifying events of World War II. This Declaration begins: "Everyone shall live free and equal in dignity and rights." In signing the Declaration, the nations of the world also undertook to help obtain the range of human rights, from freedom of conscience to a free wage, not just for their own citizens but also for those in other countries.

But human rights are too important—and vulnerable—to be left to governments. Governments will always find excuses to ignore human rights. It is ordinary people, not only in international organizations like Amnesty but also in the many national human rights organizations throughout the world, who must ensure that the Universal Declaration of Human Rights is upheld.

This book includes many examples of how ordinary people have worked for human rights. Sometimes a prisoner was released or torture stopped, other times a campaign proved to be a long struggle with little progress. Yet, however deaf and stubborn governments may appear to be, it is important to have groups and individuals determined to bring to light the prison cells and torture chambers that they would rather keep secret.

Pressure can also bring victories. On November 22, 1989, Amnesty International sent an Austrian lawyer to observe the trial of Czechoslovak dissident Jan Carnogursky. Within three weeks he was released. He later became Deputy Prime Minister and Minister of the Interior, and was put in charge of the police who had earlier locked him up for his peacefully held views!

HUMAN RIGHTS CHANGES AROUND THE GLOBE

1990 was a watershed year for human rights. The news that emerged from Eastern Europe, South America, and South

"It's not how long he's been in there, it's how many letters we've had demanding his release." **David Haldane**

Africa all fed a new optimism. The Berlin Wall had just fallen. In Chile, Augusto Pinochet, defeated in a national plebiscite, was forced to turn over the reigns of power to a civilian government. And a former Amnesty International prisoner of conscience, Vaclav Havel, became Czechoslovakia's first democratic President since the late 1940s.

Half a world away, in South Africa, Nelson Mandela—perhaps the world's most famous political prisoner—was released, and a meaningful political dialogue began on the future of that country.

But there was a downside. The vast political changes sweeping Europe unleashed nationalist tensions that had long been repressed. No one could say for certain how the new nationalist fervor would effect human rights in the region. There were violent clashes throughout Eastern Europe. In Yugoslavia, disturbances in Kosovo Province during January and February left 30 dead. Some of the republics within the

Soviet Union began to call for independence. Soviet attempts to crack down on these secessionist movements sometimes led to violence, while in other parts of the country long-hostile ethnic communities turned to force to settle their ancient animosities.

In Southeast Asia, there were extensive reports of torture in Myanmar (Burma), where a military government continued in power despite losing a national election. In the 18 months preceding the elections, the authorities arrested and detained thousands of supporters of non-violent political parties. China began to put on trial many long-term dissidents, some of whom had taken part in pro-democracy demonstrations the previous spring.

Meanwhile, in Central America, El Salvador's death squads continued their murderous activity in 1990, despite pledges by the government that steps were being taken to prevent and investigate human rights abuses.

One event overshadowed all others. On August 2, Iraq invaded Kuwait. The invasion and subsequent occupation of Kuwait resulted in a wave of serious human rights violations, and the world was witness to a military confrontation in the Persian Gulf. As war clouds gathered throughout the autumn there was growing concern for human rights, both in the Middle East and beyond.

The old year ended on a somber note. War broke out early in the new year. The wave of optimism that had brought in 1990 had dissolved into a more sober reality in 1991.

As Amnesty International gets ready to mark its 30th Anniversary, there will be no letting up in the volume or intensity of the work to be done.

THE CHALLENGE OF GROWTH

The face of Amnesty International is changing rapidly. Sometimes thought of in the past as a "western" organization, because most of its membership was located in Western Europe and North America, the organization is becoming a truly worldwide movement. In 1990, Amnesty International's membership passed the one million mark, and much of that growth came outside Amnesty's traditional base.

Today, change in Eastern Europe is opening up vast new opportunities for building a human rights community there. By the end of 1989, several Amnesty International groups were forming in the area. In December 1989 a group in Slovenia, Yugoslavia, became the first to be officially recognized by the organization. In the past two years Amnesty International groups have formed in Hungary, Poland, Czechoslovakia, Bulgaria, and Romania.

Amnesty is currently launching its first major development drive in the Soviet Union. Already there are 200 members in the USSR, in more than half a dozen centers throughout the country. In 1991 Amnesty expects to open an office in Moscow—the first non-Soviet human rights organization to gain permission to do so. Doors that have been closed to us for nearly 30 years are opening for the first time.

But growth is not limited to Eastern Europe. In Sub-Saharan Africa, Amnesty now has membership structures in five countries, with active groups in another three. In Asia, five countries have membership structures, with less formal groupings in another nine, including Pakistan and Nepal, where renewed interest was expressed in 1989.

In the Middle East and North Africa the movement has continued to consolidate and expand, with members now active in eight countries.

There is also interest in Central and South America. In that region there are now groups or members in 19 countries as well as subscribers and supporters in a further 10. The most recently created section in the area is in Uruguay, established in 1985 following a period of military rule marked by serious and wide-ranging human rights abuses.

All this growth has created the need to communicate effectively in the many languages of its membership. Both Amnesty International's Annual Report and the monthly Amnesty International newsletter now appear in the movement's official languages: Arabic, English, French and Spanish. Many research papers are published in additional languages when appropriate.

This tremendous diversity and array of talent provides the organization with a wonderful opportunity to carry the human rights message more effectively to the world in the 1990s, both at the local and global levels.

Chapter Two
PRISONERS OF CONSCIENCE

"My husband used to be a judge. In 1975, there was an attempted coup in Somalia. The President brought in laws that were undemocratic, unfair. My husband would have had to implement them, sentencing people without fair trial. So he resigned, but President Siad Barre put him under great pressure. My husband was not allowed to work or leave the country. We knew what was going to happen so, in 1976, he left Somalia.

"I wanted to join him, but they wouldn't let me. I had three children and they put me under a lot of pressure. They would come and sit on the steps of my house and look through the windows at me. This went on for two years.

"I was arrested on the morning of June 13, 1978. I was going to visit my mother, to the north of Mogadishu. A Land Rover pulled up in front of the bus and forced it to stop. Some men jumped out. They were in uniform, but I recognized them as being the same men who had harassed me at home. There were six of them to arrest just me. They were very rude and rough and humiliating.

"When we arrived, I was taken to a place I knew of. It is called 'The Hole'. Immediately I was stripped and questioned. They thought I was leaving the country, but I told them where I had been going.

"I don't remember those early days and weeks and months very well. The first day, yes. All the rest is blurred. I was unconscious a lot of the time, or I was too weak or too tired. I can only tell you how it all started. There was no real routine to the torture. I didn't know when to expect it or why. When it happened it was always at night, from nine o'clock to about three in the morning. Perhaps that's when they were bored.

"Because of Amnesty, my name was well known in different parts of the world. Later I learned that Siad Barre had received letters from Amnesty. I remember receiving one, too. All I can recall of it is that I burnt it as I was afraid that if it was found, I might have been in danger. But it was a very good thing for me. It is so important that prisoners get letters. It really does help.

"When it came to my final release, it was again because of a rumor. It was put around that I wanted to divorce my husband; this would have meant that I no longer supported him or the opposition in exile. This would have been good publicity for the government. They believed the story so much, that they quickly brought the papers for me to sign. I did this. And so I was released.

"Two day later, I escaped from Somalia. To this day I don't know how I managed it. The observers must have been asleep. I had to walk the last fifteen kilometers at night, as the area was full of soldiers. We had to walk on the exposed roots of trees and on clumps of grass to avoid the mines. It was a very long night.

"Eventually I made my way to Galdogob. When my husband arrived there, we were all together again, after so many years. I cannot tell you how I felt."

Saida Botan Elmi, Somali ex-prisoner of
conscience, released June 1984

Amnesty International's symbol is a candle surrounded by barbed wire. It is taken from the proverb, "better to light a candle than curse the darkness." Lit in 1961, the candle has come to represent all those prisoners, like Saida, whom Amnesty seeks to help.

At the heart of the Amnesty flame are the prisoners of conscience—people detained because of their beliefs, color,

"I can't remember whether I was writing a subversive novel or reading a subversive novel." **David Haldane**

sex, ethnic origin, language or religion, who have not used or advocated violence. Their imprisonment is a violation of the Universal Declaration of Human Rights, and Amnesty works for their immediate and unconditional release.

Many prisoners of conscience have tried to exercise their freedom to say what they believe, meet with whom they choose, or to go where they wish. Some are held for voicing their disagreement with government policy. Others have been imprisoned because they belong to political or religious groups outlawed by their government. Some are conscientious objectors, who are opposed to military service. Others are imprisoned simply because members of their families are political or religious activists. Some have themselves tried to publicize human rights violations in their countries.

Whatever their views, all prisoners of conscience have expressed their dissent peacefully.

Some who disagree with Amnesty argue that sometimes the freedom of the individual must be sacrificed to serve the interests of the community; others hold that the exercise of freedom of expression amounts to "pathological individualism"—a charge once made against the late Andrei Sakharov.

Amnesty, however, upholds the individual's right to non-violent freedom of conscience and belief without exception, and opposes the detention of prisoners of conscience in all cases.

WHO IS A PRISONER OF CONSCIENCE?

In many countries, it is easy to become a prisoner of conscience. If you were a dock worker in Syria, a member of the Royal Family in Ethiopia, a lay preacher in Vietnam, or a rubber tapper in Brazil, you might at one time have been adopted as a PoC by Amnesty.

Some PoCs, such as 24-year-old Wang Dan, have gained prominence in their country's struggle for human rights. A history student at Beijing University, he became a key figure in the pro-democracy movement in 1989. He was Chairman of the student Society of Contemporary Social Problems and organized 60 students to sign a petition calling for greater democracy on the campus.

After government forces attacked Tiananmen Square, Wang Dan was seen counting the dead and wounded in nearby hospitals. On June 13, a warrant was issued for his arrest as one of the twenty "most wanted" student leaders. He was arrested and apparently beaten during interrogations. He has now been sentenced to nine years imprisonment on charges of "counter-revolutionary propaganda and agitation."

Champions of human rights like Wang Dan are important to all of us. By defending those who speak out against injustice, we are also defending our own rights. However, most prisoners of conscience are not political activists or well-known dissenters; they simply hold views with which their governments disagree, or belong to a race or religion which their governments do not like.

A discussion in Prague between three firemen supposedly criticizing the general situation in Czechoslovakia resulted in a three-year prison sentence for "subversion" in 1986 for 38-year-old Ervin Motl.

Agripino Quispe, a 56-year-old shoemaker and lay protestant preacher in the Peruvian peasant community of San Pablo, was given a six-year prison term on charges of terrorism in 1985, after "confessing" under torture.

And in Sri Lanka, a ten-year-old child, Kayathiri Vino Sangaralingam, was arrested in 1987 with her mother and two older sisters. All of them later "disappeared." A Tamil herself, Kayathiri was apparently suspected of being sympathetic to the Liberation Tigers of Tamil Eelam.

HOW MANY PRISONERS ARE PoCs?

It is impossible to tell how many prisoners of conscience there are throughout the world, yet AI believes that over half the UN's member countries are currently holding prisoners of conscience.

At the end of 1990, AI was actively working on more than 3,000 prisoner cases. Clearly this work reaches just a fraction of those prisoners currently suffering unjust imprisonment.

"Pretty soon we're going to have to tell him he's adopted."
Riana Duncan

WHAT THE GOVERNMENTS SAY

Few governments openly admit that they have detained people in violation of international standards. Many governments use the cover of a threat to national security and pass "laws" which define this threat so broadly that anyone who is or is believed to be critical of official policies can be locked up. Most government officials withhold the true facts about the people they decide to detain, usually from both local and world opinion.

Others are refreshingly candid. Mahgoub el-Bedawi, the Education Minister of the Military Government of Sudan, stated in 1989:

"I don't believe there are many [political prisoners] in jail. It's only very few who oppose the Government. It is obvious: if you are in power and you are opposed, you keep your enemies or those who are opposing you in jail for a while, and when you feel you are safe and they are not opposing you, you can release them."

WHAT HAPPENS TO PRISONERS

Imprisonment can take many different forms. Most prisoners of conscience are held in prisons, camps, interrogation centers, or army barracks. Many others are held under house arrest, physically restricted by "banning" orders, or sent into internal exile in remote areas. Some have been forcibly confined to psychiatric hospitals.

Conditions for prisoners of conscience can be very harsh. Irina Ratushinskaya was sentenced to seven years hard labor and five years internal exile in the USSR—the maximum possible punishment for anti-Soviet agitation and propaganda. Irina's sentence was, in the words of her husband, human rights activist Igor Gerashchenko, "based on five poems as remote from politics as the Lord's Prayer." Nonetheless, at the age of 28, she became the youngest woman to be incarcerated in the Small Zone, a special unit for women political prisoners in Mordovia. It constituted the harshest regime of imprisonment allowed for women under Soviet law.

For four years, Irina endured a nightmarish existence of undernourishment, intense cold, abuse from camp authorities, detention in isolation cells, and other punishments which seriously undermined her health. At 32, she suffered from extremely high blood pressure, angina, blackouts, and severe eye pain. There were no facilities at the camp to treat her.

Irina was finally released in October 1986. Her fellow-prisoners were also freed in the ensuing months and the Small Zone has been closed.

CAMPAIGNING FOR PRISONERS

The amount of information reaching the International Secretariat about individual prisoners varies considerably. In some cases, such as those of well-known politicians, writers, or eminent scientists, full biographical details are available. In other cases, an AI delegation may gather data firsthand.

More often, however, very little is known about the prisoner. He or she may have come from a remote village with poor roads or means of communication or may be held incommunicado in an isolated prison. Relatives may also have been arrested and unable to help, or the fear of reprisals may keep them silent. Most prisoners do not know that Amnesty exists and may doubt its ability to help them even if they do.

Information about prisoners reaches Amnesty by many different paths. It may be provided by prisoners themselves, by their families, by lawyers who defend them, by doctors who attend them, by refugees, or by religious bodies. Details also come from the world media, and from Amnesty delegates who are sent on missions to collect specific information on a case or country.

All the information is carefully examined and cross-checked, biographical and legal data is collected, and a careful assessment is made of each case, taking into account the changing politics and laws of each country.

WORKING ON A CASE

If it appears that a prisoner is in fact being held for her or his conscientiously held beliefs, and has not used or advocated violence, the prisoner will be "adopted" by an Amnesty group that has volunteered to work on her or his behalf.

"I tried to form a trade union—and you?" **Len Spencer**

If Amnesty believes someone may be a prisoner of conscience but lacks conclusive evidence of this, the case may be assigned to an AI group for investigation. The group then attempts to obtain further information about the case. If this becomes available, or if the authorities fail to provide adequate information to justify the prisoner's detention, the case may be changed to adoption. But some cases do remain investigation cases for a long time.

As mentioned earlier, in order to safeguard Amnesty's impartiality groups do not work on behalf of prisoners held in their own countries. This rule also protects Amnesty members who work in countries where they may be endangered. Every effort is also made to achieve a political, geographical, and ideological balance in the work groups undertake.

Sometimes, groups are fortunate enough to make contact with "their" prisoners, and to communicate directly with them.

Boris Perchatkin, a prominent activist within the "unofficial" Soviet Pentecostalist church, was arrested on August 18, 1980, after Soviet authorities searched his house and found quantities of religious literature as well as some correspondence from abroad. Sentenced to two years imprisonment for "anti-Soviet slander," he was sent to serve his term at the Sverdlovsk camp in the Urals.

A Southern California group received Perchatkin's prison dossier in February 1982 and began the long and often frustrating campaign to gain his freedom. Hundreds of letters were sent to the various officials who controlled his destiny, with little response during his prison term.

Soviet authorities released Perchatkin in August 1982, only to arrest him again six months later on an obscure charge. The group asked the International Secretariat in London for permission to intervene on his behalf again and once again began writing to Soviet authorities. In August 1984, he was released. But the group decided to continue writing as private citizens to gain his permission to emigrate.

After years of frustration, imprisonment, and official harassment, Perchatkin finally got his wish. He and his family, including eight children, left the Soviet Union for the United States in August 1988. Shortly after their arrival, a member of the group received a telephone call notifying them that the Perchatkin family had settled in the Springfield, Massachusetts area.

The group decided to have a fundraiser on the family's behalf and requested a picture of Perchatkin for the reception. At which point their contact said, "You don't need a picture, I can send Boris!"

With the combined help of Pentecostal churches in Springfield and California, Perchatkin was able to travel west and meet with the Southern California group. He was accompanied by his wife and several other guests, including Anatoly Kabinov, another former Soviet prisoner unofficially sponsored by the group. "It was a dream we never thought would come true," a member said.

KEEPING UP THE PRESSURE

In 1990, there was good news to report. The United States section was working on only 31 cases which had been adopted over 10 years, and only 56 cases had been on the books for more than five years. In December 1989, US groups were working on behalf of 480 individual cases.

One obvious reason for this improvement is that many long-term cases in the former German Democratic Republic, the USSR and throughout Eastern Europe have now been closed. However, in other countries, such as Ethiopia and Somalia, the release of long-term prisoners has been followed by a return to repressive force and torture, and an influx of newly adopted prisoners.

It is difficult for a group to work for a prisoner's release with little information and no feedback from the government concerned. It is a mark of the commitment of Amnesty's many groups that they do not give up hope for long-term prisoners, maintaining the consistent pressure which is essential in such cases.

> "If there's lots of pressure—like from Amnesty International or some foreign countries—then we might pass them on to a judge, but if there's no pressure, then they're dead."
>
> *A Salvadoran torturer*

WHAT THE PRISONERS SAY

On their release, many prisoners of conscience write to those who campaigned for their freedom, describing what the support of strangers has meant to them.

> "I am free," wrote one prisoner. "I have just been freed this evening. I assure you that I owe my freedom to you. I survived thanks to you. It is true that one must never despair in life. This victory is completely yours, you who have been untiring workers. From this moment, a new page in my life has been turned."

Other former prisoners have written:

"The only daylight that entered my cell was through a small opening at the top of one wall. One day, the door to my cell opened, and the guard tossed in a crumpled piece of paper. It said simply, 'Constantino, do not be discouraged; we know you are alive.' It was signed 'Monica' and had the Amnesty International candle on it. These words saved my life and my sanity. Eight months later I was set free."

Constantino Coronel, former prisoner of
conscience, Paraguay

"We could always tell when international protests were taking place . . . the food rations increased and the beatings were fewer. Letters from abroad were translated and passed around from cell to cell . . . ."

Released prisoner, Vietnam

"A political prisoner comes to know about your work on his behalf usually only indirectly, from the sarcastic remarks of his jailers or from pieces of information communicated to him by members of his family in their strictly censored letters. But it is enough to give him a wonderful feeling that he is not completely forgotten after all, that somebody cares."

Karel Kyncl, former prisoner of conscience,
Czechoslovakia

Chapter Three

TORTURE AND CRUEL, INHUMAN, AND DEGRADING TREATMENT

Here the sweet and the beautiful,
Are a kick in the teeth and pain,
What leads to convulsions Mother:
The roughin' up, the electric charge.
We are light bulbs Mother,
Light bulbs that scream.
But lightless, Mother, lightless.

Hugo Diaz

"Among the rights universally proclaimed by all nations . . . is the right to be free of physical torture. Indeed, for purposes of civil liability, the torturer has become—like the pirate and slave trader before him—*hostis humani generis,* an enemy of mankind."

Judge Irving Kaufman

AN UNSPEAKABLE PRACTICE

Torture, as defined by the 1949 Geneva Convention, is "the deliberate, systematic or wanton infliction of physical and mental suffering by one or more persons acting alone or on the orders of an authority, to force another person to yield information, to make a confession, or for any other reason which is an outrage to personal dignity."

To most people, torture is a repugnant and unspeakable practice. Yet during the 1980s, torture and ill-treatment of prisoners was reported from over 90 countries—more than half the countries of the world. These torturing nations cover all five continents and include liberal democracies as well as totalitarian regimes.

A LITANY OF PAIN

Torture is no modern plague. Throughout history, rulers and governments of all political shades have used torture when it was expedient for them to do so. Under the Roman Empire, for example, civil and criminal courts sanctioned torture as a means of extorting confessions in trials of treason or sorcery, and permitted masters to use torture to discipline slaves. During the Middle Ages, suspected heretics were racked, scourged, and burned by representatives of the Inquisition in order to make them recant. In the sixteenth century, Spanish Conquistadors tortured captive Native Americans in their thirst for gold, while Englishmen led raiding parties on African villages to capture slaves, often torturing village leaders to discover the whereabouts of other villagers.

The litany of pain reverberates through our own century to the present day: in the concentration camps of Hitler, the Gulag Archipelago and psychiatric wards of Stalin and his successors, Pol Pot's killing fields, the detention centers of Idi Amin, Pinochet, Mao, Khomeini, Ceausescu . . . . The list appears endless.

THE ETHICS OF TORTURE

Are there ever occasions where torture is justified? Its apologists argue that there are, for instance when its use protects an innocent population from terrorist attack.

One argument commonly used is this one. A man detained by the police has planted a bomb in a New York store. If it goes off, a hundred people will die. He knows where the bomb is, but will not tell. Should he be tortured? Can we balance the pain of one person against the lives of many?

From the point of view of society, the arguments for allowing torture in "special circumstances" are dangerous and naïve. Once justified and allowed for the narrower purpose of combating political violence, torture can be used for a wider range of purposes against an increasing proportion of the population. This is reflected in statements from torturers, like the one below.

> "The objective was to obtain a confession from the detainee, purely and simply. The authorities constantly enjoined on us the need to obtain confessions in order to save the lives of military personnel who might be in danger of attack by revolutionary groups .... However, subsequently the idea began to lose its force and changed into the application of torture for its own sake, as part of a routine, and also as an act of vengeance against the detainee."
>
> *Julio Cesar Cooper,*
> *Uruguayan Army torturer*

OBJECTIVES OF TORTURE

Torture is most often used by governments as an integral part of their security strategy. If threatened by guerrillas, a government may condone torture as a means of extracting vital logistical information from captured insurgents. The intimidation of rural populations through torture and killings has often been used to bring the people or areas of land under government control. The majority of the victims have no security information to give away; they serve only as a grim message to others not to oppose the government.

Torture is often used specifically to intimidate the victim and other potential dissidents, and discourage them from further political activity. Students detained for demonstrating or leafleting in the Republic of Korea have been routinely tortured and beaten at police stations, then released without charge.

Another reason is to obtain confessions as primary evidence against a detainee. In Northern Ireland, for example, the increased number of assaults made during interrogation from

1976 onward was partly the result of a British government security strategy to obtain confessions that could be used in court.

Torture and ill treatment are also used as punishments, sometimes in addition to prison sentences. Caning, flogging and, in a few countries, amputation are judicially prescribed. Prisoners on hunger strikes against harsh prison conditions or in protest against their own torture have been severely beaten in the Republic of Korea.

Isolated incidents of torture do occur without government approval. However, governments are not blameless if they fail to investigate such alleged abuses of authority. Their failure to investigate the offense and discipline the offender is often taken as a signal by the security agent or agency involved that the abuses are officially tolerated.

WHAT MAKES A TORTURER?

The common image of a torturer is of an inhuman, twisted personality, a sadist who takes pleasure in inflicting pain on his victim. Although this may be true in a number of cases, the terrifying reality is that, given the right circumstances, anyone can become a torturer. The *chief* prerequisite is unconditional obedience to authority:

> "The essence of obedience consists in the fact that a person comes to view himself as the instrument for carrying out another person's wishes, and he therefore no longer regards himself as responsible for his actions."
> *Stanley Milgram, US psychologist*

In the making of the modern torturer such obedience is rigorously enforced. The testimony of former torturers from various countries, including Argentina, Uruguay, and Paraguay, has allowed us to build a picture of the training they undergo to turn them into tools of repression. However, the most comprehensive accounts of the making of a torturer come from testimony given in the trial of a group of Greek torturers in 1974, following the fall of the military regime earlier that year.

Nick Baker

After basic training, young conscripts from known anti-communist families were selected for special training for the military police, the ESA. Further screening produced the chosen few to be trained as torturers. A large part of their training consisted of beating and being beaten by fellow conscripts.

"It's nothing, Mr. Chairman," said former Corporal Themistoklis Vlochaitis, a prosecution witness, "to give someone five blows when you've received sixty from your comrades."

The officers who trained these conscripts ordered them to eat the straps of their berets, to kneel and swear allegiance to portraits of their commanding officers, and to perform demeaning sexual acts in front of other soldiers. After ideological indoctrination and psychological conditioning, the conscripts were assigned first to guard prisoners, then to arrest suspects, and finally to torture them. Hesitation to torture led to ridicule, more beatings, threats of transfer and loss of privileges, as well as threats to the economic livelihood of the conscript's family.

> "I was caught up in a machine and became a tool without any will of my own to resist. I remember Spanos threatening a soldier that he would ruin his family. The next day the boy began to beat prisoners . . . ."

> "I feel the need to tell this respected tribunal and the Greek people that I am a human being like you, like your neighbor's son, like a friend."
> *Testimonies from two Greek torturers*

PRECONDITIONS FOR TORTURE

Torture most often occurs during a detainee's first days in custody. These vulnerable hours are usually spent incommunicado, when the security forces have total control over the fate of the detainee, denying access to relatives, lawyers, or an independent doctor. Some detainees are held in secret, their whereabouts known only to their captors. The authorities may deny that certain detainees are held, making it easier to torture or kill them, or to make them "disappear."

The suspension of habeas corpus and other legal remedies, trials of political detainees in military courts, the lack of independent means to examine and record a prisoner's medical condition—all these conditions allow the security forces to conceal evidence of torture from lawyers, civilian magistrates, independent doctors, and others who would be capable of taking action against their illegal activities.

Trial procedures that do not exclude from evidence statements extracted under torture or during long periods of incommunicado detention reinforce the culture of torture. Some governments refuse to investigate allegations of torture, or deny that torture occurs, even in the face of mounting evidence of deaths in custody, or they obstruct independent domestic or international investigations, and provide immunity to alleged torturers from criminal and civil prosecution.

THE FIGHT AGAINST TORTURE

For centuries, torture was an integral part of the legal process in many countries. In Europe it was not completely forbidden by law until 1808, when Napoleon's *Code d'Instruction Criminelle* ended secret juristic procedures. As recognition of the inherent rights and duties of citizens grew in the late eighteenth and early nineteenth centuries, the barbarity of torture came to be officially recognized, and many countries outlawed it.

Since then, several national and international charters and declarations have reinforced Napoleon's codes. A key point was the Declaration of Human Rights adopted by the United Nations General Assembly in 1948. The UN Declaration expressly stated in Article 5 that "No one shall be subject to torture or to cruel, inhuman, or degrading treatment or punishment."

Today, the legal foundation for the prohibition of torture rests on two sources of international law: treaties and international custom. The Geneva Conventions, the International Covenant on Civil and Political Rights, the UN Convention Against Torture, and regional human rights conventions are legally binding on the states that ratify them.

The Convention Against Torture came into force on June 26, 1987, ratified by twenty nations. By January 1990, fifty countries had ratified the convention and an additional 22, including the United States, had signed it, thereby proclaiming their intent to ratify. At the end of 1990, the Senate voted in favor of ratification, legally binding the United States Government to uphold the treaty.

However, words and pledges are never enough in themselves. In early 1988, for example, Turkey signed and ratified both the United Nations Convention against Torture and the European Convention for the Prevention of Torture. The 1982 Turkish Constitution prohibits torture and the penal code provides for torturers to be punished. The Turkish Government has stated frequently that it does not condone the use of torture. The reality is somewhat different:

> "They were asking who the documents belonged to. They made us hold hands, tied them together and poured water over them. They applied electricity to the little fingers of my left hand and his right hand. They asked the same and other questions, but did not get the answers they wanted ....
>
> "Now our screams became a choir. They took a break and got Perihan and asked her who the documents belonged to. She said she did not know. Now they made all three of us hold hands and placed us side by side.
>
> "Hasan was on the right side, I was on the left and Perihan in the middle. The cables were fixed to one another.... Again we got the shocks ....
>
> "Hasan and I screamed. Perihan first kept silent, later she reacted to the current as well. Screams and more screams, mixing with each other. Now the choir was complete."
>
> *Former torture victim from Turkey*

Over a quarter of a million people have been arrested on political grounds in Turkey since 1980, and almost all of them have been tortured.

Governments must be made to realize that torture is unacceptable in any form and for any reason. The most effective weapon against torture is public opinion. National and international human rights groups play a vital role in this regard by collecting evidence of government-sponsored torture. By bringing it to the world's attention they can shame governments into prohibiting its use.

In December, 1972, Amnesty launched its first Campaign Against Torture specifically to arouse public awareness. As part of the Campaign, a petition was circulated in thirty languages calling upon the General Assembly of the UN "to outlaw immediately the torture of prisoners throughout the world." By the end of 1973, more than one million people had signed. During the campaign and subsequent to it, Amnesty developed a number of techniques aimed at putting pressure on governments who use torture to cease this practice.

One of the most powerful of these anti-torture mechanisms is the Urgent Action program. Amnesty members from around the world are mobilized to send letters, telexes, and telegrams to the appropriate authorities as soon as the International Secretariat, Amnesty's research headquarters, learns that a prisoner is at risk of being tortured. Initially used in 1973 to prevent the possible torture of a Brazilian academic who had been arrested by the military police and subsequently "disappeared," the technique today is used in cases covering the entire range of Amnesty's concerns.

On November 22, 1986, Simon Farisani, the Dean of the Evangelical Lutheran Church in the Venda "homeland" and a former PoC, was arrested by the South African security services. On two former occasions Farisani had been tortured while in detention. Just five hours after his arrest a stream of telexes were being sent to the South African Government asking for assurances of his safety. He was released unharmed on January 30, 1987.

HOW TO IDENTIFY THUGS, HOOLIGANS & RUFFIANS in CHINA: HE IS IN THE CHAIR

Jeff Danziger in the Christian Science Monitor © 1989 TCSPS

Jeff Danziger

Many of the techniques and instruments used by torturers to perpetrate their crimes in one country have been imported from another. Over the last ten years Amnesty has endeavored to expose and halt this transfer of repressive technology.

The use of electricity in torture is worldwide. One device, popular with security forces in Latin America, is called the *picana electrica*—the electric shock baton. In 1982, the discovery of electric shock batons on display at the British Army Equipment Exhibition produced a public outcry. These protests secured a government undertaking that the display of this equipment would not be permitted in future Ministry of Defense-sponsored exhibitions. The government also reaffirmed its assurance that export licenses would not be granted for tools likely to be used for internal repression or to violate human rights.

THE WIDE NET OF TORTURE

Though only a relatively few individuals may be directly involved in the process of torture as torturers, many more can become enmeshed indirectly. Judges, lawyers, or policemen who look the other way as abuses are committed must share the guilt of the torturer. It is, however, the involvement of physicians, psychiatrists, and nurses which is especially troubling and abhorrent.

Medical personnel may participate in torture merely by providing torturers with assistance which appears to be within the scope of their proper medical duties. For example, physicians employed to examine or treat prisoners may only slowly realize that they have become accessories to torture, lending legitimacy to it by their presence in the torture cell, by giving torturers information about the physical condition of their victims, or by resuscitating victims so that they may be tortured again.

Physicians may also cooperate indirectly by failing to seek out or report evidence of torture found in medical examinations or autopsies. From such indirect involvement, medical personnel have sometimes moved to direct action: doctors have acted as expert advisers on torture techniques, or have become torturers themselves. In the early seventies medical personnel working with the Chilean secret police administered overdoses of cyclophosphamide to some detainees resulting in death from hemorrhaging into the bladder.

To prevent such debasement of their profession, national and international medical associations have attempted to construct and enforce ethical codes prohibiting any involvement of medical personnel in torture. Amnesty and other human rights organizations have constantly endeavored to ensure that they are maintained.

TORTURE AND REHABILITATION

"The trade of the torturer is one of physically and mentally violating his victims until body and mind have been refashioned to the shape that satisfies the torturer and his masters."

Eric Baker, a founding member of Amnesty

Many hundreds die every year as a result of the injuries they have received from torture, yet many more survive, broken by their ordeal both mentally and physically. Torture destroys one's sense of safety and the ability to trust the individual sitting next to you not to harm you.

Today, in more than 50 countries around the world, medical centers exist whose sole function is to undo the work of the torturer: to help rehabilitate torture victims, help them realize they are survivors and no longer victims.

While the physical injuries may heal quickly with proper treatment, the emotional ones may linger, or never heal.

In addition to terrible physical damage, many victims of torture suffer a number of psychological symptoms similar to the Post-traumatic Stress Disorder experienced by survivors of the Holocaust or soldiers who fought in the Vietnam War. Such survivors commonly exhibit anxiety, insomnia, stomach ulcers, lack of menstruation in women, and impotence in men. Many suffer from flashbacks, where a particular sight or sound can induce a sensation that they are back in the torture chamber. Rehabilitation assists the survivor to control these behavioral consequences of torture.

Although methods of dealing with the psychological trauma

of torture differ from center to center, almost all employ some form of testimony as a first step. When a survivor is able to discuss or write what occurred in detail, the incidents cease to be a deep, burning wound. Sharing their experiences with other survivors enables individuals to realize that others have also been through similar ordeals, and that they are not abnormal.

In many cases, treatment must also eliminate negative behaviors that develop. Self-abuse and the abuse of others, both mental and physical, are normal reactions to torture.

Although rehabilitation work is outside Amnesty's direct mandate, many such centers work closely with Amnesty sections and groups, and the organization frequently refers refugees who have suffered torture to them. Through its relief work Amnesty helps released PoCs and former torture victims to rebuild their lives. In an increasing number of cases, Amnesty funds and arranges for the medical treatment of such victims of human rights abuse.

Amnesty has, for example, contributed to a clinic in Pakistan which provides medical and psychiatric treatment for Afghan torture victims who have fled there as refugees.

Often these centers have arisen as a result of initiatives by Amnesty. This was the case with the International Rehabilitation Center for Torture Victims (RCT), the first such rehabilitation center established. It was founded in Denmark in 1982 by ex-members of the Danish Amnesty Medical Group led by Dr. Inge Kemp Genefke following an international meeting on the issue held by AI in Stockholm. Similarly, in the UK the Medical Foundation for the Care of Victims of Torture, formed in December 1985, evolved out of the work of the British Section Medical Group.

In the United States there are currently two torture rehabilitation centers. One, the Center for the Victims of Torture, was established in Minneapolis in 1985. The other, the Marjorie Kovler Center for the Treatment of Survivors of Torture, is based in Chicago. The Minneapolis center says it cared for 240 patients in 1990, 42 percent of whom were from Africa, 16 percent from Latin America, 13 percent from the Middle East, 12 percent from South-East Asia, 8 percent from Europe, and 5 percent were Holocaust survivors.

Although not established as a formal rehabilitation center,

Survivors International of Northern California assists the survivors of torture through public education, training and research, and by providing appropriate referral, treatment, and recovery programs. Survivors International trains and assigns volunteers to work on a one-to-one basis with survivors to help them acquire new skills. Through help in acquiring what we may take for granted—a language, a driver's license, a medical referral—survivors learn that help *is* available, and that they are not helpless, two objectives of torture. Most treatment available in the United States, however, is through individual doctors specializing in torture rehabilitation.

As in some other centers worldwide, treatment at the RCT in Denmark and at the British Medical Foundation is multidisciplinary and holistic. The approach is flexible, varying from case to case and from center to center, but generally comprises three components. First, staff at the centers use psychotherapy and physiotherapy and, where necessary, treat the physical scars of torture. Frequently injured areas of the body include the head (particularly the ears and mouth), the soles of the feet, and the joints. Sexual torture of both sexes, including rape, is also common.

Second, whenever possible, personnel provide counseling for family members while they treat the victim—for it is vital to maintain the family. Third, the staff attempt to provide a therapeutic environment that does not evoke memories of past torture for victims. They take care that treatment situations do not mimic torture experiences: an electrocardiogram can strike terror into someone who suffered electrical torture; a rectal examination can remind victims of a sexual attack; giving a blood sample can be deeply traumatic for someone tortured with needles. White coats and the more obvious trappings of medical authority are also avoided.

> "They regard any figure in authority with suspicion. This may be compounded by the patient's previous knowledge of a doctor—perhaps one who participated in the torture, who was employed to remove traces of injury or to prescribe pauses (in the torture sessions)."
>
> *Dr. Brian Fisher,*
> *Amnesty British Medical Group*

"The body is the point of access that the torturer has to an individual's mind. Every physical scar has an emotional scar."

John Schlapobersky, physiotherapist and group analyst with the Amnesty British Medical Group

A study carried out by the Seattle-based South American Refugee Program in conjunction with Amnesty International found that many victims of torture find it difficult to reestablish relations with their spouses or to discipline children, show affection, or make decisions. Indeed, torturers often deliberately set out to destroy the family. Jacobo Timerman, himself a former prisoner of the Argentinian military, wrote in his prison memoir, *Prisoner Without a Name, Cell Without a Number* (Knopf, New York, 1981):

"Nothing can compare to those family groups who were tortured ... together.... The entire affective world, constructed over the years with utmost difficulty, collapses with a kick in the father's genitals, a smack in the mother's face, an obscene insult to the sister, or the sexual violation of the daughter. Suddenly an entire culture based on familial love, devotion, the capacity for mutual sacrifice, collapses. Nothing is possible in such a universe and that is precisely what the torturers know."

For some the effects of torture are unbearable, and suicide is a not uncommon result of torture. However, despite all they have been through, "these people are attempting to be happy," says Dr. Marlinda Freire, a Chilean-born psychiatrist associate with the Canadian Center for Victims of Torture. "They can go through extreme, devastating experiences and recover enough to integrate the experience and have some share of happiness again."

Chapter Four
THE DEATH PENALTY

"Some have to be carried tied to a chair, others dragged to the trap, limp, bowels open, arms pinioned to the back, like animals, and still other things happen which should happen only in nightmare dreams. . . ."

Arthur Koestler

"It is curious, but till that moment I had never realized what it means to destroy a healthy, conscious man. When I saw the prisoner step aside to avoid the puddle I saw the mystery, the unspeakable wrongness, of cutting a life short when it is in full tide. This man was not dying, he was alive just as we are alive . . . . His eyes saw the yellow gravel and the grey walls, and his brain still remembered, foresaw, reasoned—even about puddles. He and we were a party of men walking together, seeing, hearing feeling, understanding the same world; and in two minutes, with a sudden snap, one of us would be gone—one mind less, one world less."

George Orwell

THE CASE OF JEROME BOWDEN

Jerome Bowden, a mentally disabled black man aged 33, was executed in Georgia in June 1986 for the murder of a white woman 10 years earlier during a robbery.

His execution came a day after a state-hired psychologist had conducted a three-hour IQ test on him in prison and had effectively found that his average score of 65 was not low enough for him to be spared electrocution. Defense lawyers had no opportunity to challenge the psychologist's findings.

Jerome Bowden was sentenced to death by a jury from which the prosecutor had peremptorily excluded all blacks, even though the trial was held in a region of the state with a 34 percent black population.

Such a jury selection procedure was later ruled unconstitutional by the Supreme Court in another case. Jerome Bowden could have won a stay of execution after this ruling but his principal trial lawyer had failed to object to the procedure, thereby waiving his client's right to raise this at a later stage. His lawyer had never handled a criminal case of any kind before being appointed by the court to defend Jerome Bowden.

Jerome Bowden was convicted partly on the evidence of his own alleged confession that he had participated in the crime and partly on the testimony of a co-defendant. It was not established which of the two had been the actual killer. The co-defendant was sentenced to life imprisonment at a separate trial.

A request by Jerome Bowden for psychiatric help in testing his mental competence to stand trial was refused by the trial judge. His lawyer then withdrew an insanity claim on his behalf. This meant that not only was the jury never shown that Jerome Bowden was mentally disabled, but he had also waived his right to raise the insanity issue afterward. His case would otherwise have been reviewed in the light of a February 1985 Supreme Court ruling that states must provide indigent defendants with psychiatric assistance in preparing an insanity defense if they could show that their sanity at the time of the offense was a significant factor at trial.

Jerome Bowden was reported to have the mental age of a 12-year-old. His appeal lawyers said he had no comprehension of his conviction or of death as a punishment. One of them stated: "He cannot imagine his non-existence. Carrying out a sentence of execution against such a person would be a meaningless act of vengeance."

Jerome Bowden's execution was first set for June 18, 1986, but eight hours before he was due to die, Georgia's Board of Pardons and Paroles granted a stay of up to 90 days pending

Jeff Danziger in the Christian Science Monitor © 1990 TCSPS

Jeff Danziger

an evaluation of his mental capacity. Six days later the stay was lifted—the day after the board had received the report of a psychologist who had examined the prisoner on its behalf. The psychologist found his IQ to be 65. A member of the board is reported to have indicated later that Jerome Bowden would only have been institutionalized if his IQ rating had been lower than 45.

Observers have questioned the validity of the board's psychological evaluation, which was reached on the basis of a single test.

A spokesperson for the local branch of the American Civil Liberties Union said the prisoner's IQ of 65 would have entitled him to a full disability pension from the US Social Security.

"If your IQ is 65 or lower, you're non-functioning in our 20th century society—but you're smart enough to be killed," she said.

THE ARGUMENT IN FAVOR OF ABOLITION

The time has come to abolish the death penalty worldwide. The case for abolition becomes more compelling with each passing year. Everywhere, experience shows that executions brutalize those involved in the process. Nowhere has it been shown that the death penalty has any special power to reduce crime or political violence. In country after country, it is used disproportionately against the poor, or against racial or ethnic minorities. It is often used as a tool of political repression. It is imposed and inflicted arbitrarily. It is an irrevocable punishment, resulting inevitably in the execution of people innocent of any crime, and it is a violation of fundamental human rights.

Over the past decade an average of at least one country a year has abolished the death penalty, affirming respect for human life and dignity. Yet too many governments still believe that they can solve urgent social or political problems by executing a few or even hundreds of their citizens.

The death penalty, carried out in the name of a nation's entire population, involves everyone. Everyone should be aware of what the death penalty is, how it is used, how it affects them, how it violates fundamental rights.

HUMAN RIGHTS AND THE DEATH PENALTY

The death penalty is the premeditated and cold-blooded killing of a human being by the state. The state can exercise no greater power over a person than that of deliberately depriving him or her of life. At the heart of the case for abolition, therefore, is the question of whether the state has the right to do so.

When the world's nations came together four decades ago to found the United Nations, few reminders were needed of what could happen when a state believed that there was no limit to what it might do to a human being. The staggering extent of state brutality and terror during World War II, and the consequences for people throughout the world, were still unfolding in December 1948, when the UN General Assembly adopted without dissent the Universal Declaration of Human Rights.

The Universal Declaration is a pledge among nations to promote fundamental rights as the foundation of freedom, justice, and peace. The rights it proclaims are inherent in every human being. They are not privileges that may be granted by governments for good behavior and withdrawn for bad behavior. Fundamental human rights limit what a state may do to a man, woman, or child.

No matter what reason a government gives for executing prisoners and what method of execution is used, the death penalty cannot be separated from the issue of human rights. The movement for abolition cannot be separated from the movement for human rights.

THE CRUELTY OF THE DEATH PENALTY

The Universal Declaration recognizes each person's right to life, and categorically states further that "No one shall be subjected to torture or to cruel, inhuman, or degrading treatment or punishment." In Amnesty International's view the death penalty violates these rights.

Self-defense may be held to justify, in some cases, the taking of life by state officials; for example, when a country is locked in warfare (international or civil) or when law-enforcement officials must act immediately to save their own lives or those of others. Even in such situations the use of lethal force is limited by internationally accepted legal safeguards to inhibit abuse. It is a use of force that may only be used to counter the immediate damage that may result from force used by others.

The death penalty, however, is not an act of self-defense against an immediate threat to life. It is the premeditated killing of a prisoner who could be dealt with equally well by less harsh means.

There can never be a justification for torture or for cruel, inhuman, or degrading treatment or punishment. The cruelty of the death penalty is evident. Like torture, an execution constitutes an extreme physical and mental assault on a person already rendered helpless by government authorities.

If hanging a woman by her arms until she experiences excruciating pain is rightly condemned as torture, how does one describe hanging her by the neck until she is dead? If administering 100 volts of electricity to the most sensitive parts of a man's body evokes disgust, what is the appropriate reaction to the administration of 2,000 volts to his body in order to kill him? If a pistol held to the head or a chemical substance injected to cause protracted suffering are clearly instruments of torture, how should they be identified when used to kill by shooting or lethal injection? Does the interpolation of legal process in these cruelties make their inhumanity justifiable?

The physical pain caused by the action of killing a human being cannot be quantified. Nor can the psychological suffering caused by foreknowledge of death at the hands of the state. Whether a death sentence is carried out 6 minutes after a summary trial, 6 weeks after a mass trial, or 16 years after lengthy legal proceedings, the person executed is subjected to uniquely cruel, inhuman, and degrading treatment and punishment.

The death penalty may also include other human rights violations. When a state jails people solely because of their beliefs, it violates the right to freedom of belief and expression. The death penalty is sometimes used to permanently silence political opponents or to eliminate "troublesome" individuals. Whenever and wherever used, it finally and unalterably ends a person's right to hold opinions and to speak freely, because it takes that person's life.

When a state convicts prisoners without affording them a fair trial, it denies the right to due process and equality before the law. The irrevocable punishment of death removes not only the victim's right to seek legal redress for wrongful conviction, but also the judicial system's capacity to correct its errors.

Like killings which take place outside the law, the death penalty denies the value of human life. By violating the right to life, it removes the foundation for the realization of all rights enshrined in the Universal Declaration of Human Rights.

As the Human Rights Committee set up under the International Covenant on Civil and Political Rights has recognized, "The right to life ... is the supreme right from which no derogation is permitted even in time of public emergency which threatens the life of the nation...." In a general comment on Article 6 of the Covenant issued in 1982, the Committee concluded that "all measures of abolition [of the death penalty] should be considered as progress in the enjoyment of the right to life within the meaning of Article 40."

Many governments have recognized that the death penalty cannot be reconciled with respect for human rights. The UN has declared itself in favor of abolition, and over 40 percent of all countries have abolished the death penalty in law or in practice.

WHY THE STATE KILLS

However, some 92 countries retain and use the death penalty. Unlike torture, "disappearances," and extrajudicial executions, most judicial executions are not carried out in secret or denied by government authorities. Executions are often announced in advance. In some countries they are carried out in public or before a group of invited observers.

No government publicly admits to torture or other grave violations of human rights, although privately some officials may seek to justify such abuses in the name of the "greater good." But retentionist governments, those that keep the death penalty, for the most part openly admit to using it. They do not so much deny its cruelty as attempt to justify its use, and the arguments they use publicly to justify the death penalty resemble those that are used in private to justify other, secret abuses.

The most common justification offered is that, terrible as it is, the death penalty is necessary; it may be necessary only temporarily, but, it is argued, only the death penalty can meet a particular need of society. And whatever that need may be, it is claimed to be so great that it justifies the cruel punishment of death.

The particular needs claimed to be served by the death penalty differ from time to time and from society to society. In some countries the penalty is considered legitimate as a means of preventing or punishing the crime of murder. Elsewhere, it may be deemed necessary to stop drug-trafficking, acts of political terror, economic corruption, or adultery. In yet other countries, it is used to eliminate those seen as posing a political threat to the authorities.

Once one state uses the death penalty for any reason, it becomes easier for other states to use it with an appearance of legitimacy for whatever reasons they may choose. If the death penalty can be justified for one offense, justifications can always be found for it to be used for other offenses.

Whatever rationalization is used, the idea that a government can justify a punishment as cruel as death contradicts the very concept of human rights. The significance of human rights is precisely that some measures may never be used to protect society because their use violates the very values which make society worth protecting. When this essential distinction between appropriate and inappropriate means is set aside in the name of some "greater good," all rights are vulnerable and all individuals are threatened.

The death penalty, as a violation of fundamental human rights, would be wrong even if it could be shown that it uniquely met a vital social need. What makes the use of the penalty even more indefensible and the case for its abolition even more compelling is that it has never been shown to have any special power to meet any genuine social need.

Nick Baker

Countless men and women have been executed for the purpose of preventing crime, especially the crime of murder. Yet, study after study in diverse countries has failed to find convincing evidence that the death penalty has any unique capacity to deter others from committing particular crimes. A survey of research findings on the relation between the death penalty and homicide rates, conducted for the UN in 1988, concluded that "this research has failed to provide scientific proof that executions have a greater deterrent effect than life imprisonment. Such proof is unlikely to be forthcoming. The evidence as a whole still gives no positive support to the deterrent hypothesis."

Undeniably, by permanently "incapacitating" a prisoner, the death penalty prevents that person from repeating the crime. But there is no way to be sure that the prisoner would indeed have repeated the crime if allowed to live, nor is there any need to violate the prisoner's right to life for the purpose of incapacitation: dangerous offenders can be kept safely away from the public without resorting to execution, as shown by the experience of many abolitionist countries.

Nor is there evidence that the threat of the death penalty will prevent politically motivated crimes or acts of terror. If anything, the possibility of political martyrdom through execution may encourage people to commit such crimes.

Every society seeks protection from crime. But, far from being a solution, the death penalty gives the *erroneous* impression that "firm measures" are being taken against crime. It diverts attention from the more complex measures which are really needed.

"... the constant emphasis on capital punishment is preventing us from giving real attention and real resources to the problems of crime in a modern democracy.... We must recognize that if we really are to tackle the penal problems of the country we must turn our attention to that, instead of automatically saying that the answer is hanging or flogging."

Edward Heath, former Prime Minister of the United Kingdom, speaking in a debate on the death penalty in the House of Commons on July 13, 1983.

Once the arguments of deterrence and incapacitation are removed, we are left with a more emotional, deep-seated justification for the death penalty: that it is fair retribution for the particular crime committed. According to this argument, certain people deserve to be killed as repayment for the evil they have done—that there are crimes so offensive that killing the offender is the only just response.

It is a powerful argument. It is also one which, if valid, would invalidate the basis for human rights. If a person who commits a terrible act "deserves" the cruelty of death, why don't others, for similar reasons, "deserve" to be tortured, or imprisoned without trial, or simply shot on sight? It is central to fundamental human rights that they are inalienable: they may not be taken away even if a person commits the most atrocious crimes. Human rights apply to the worst of us as well as to the best of us, which is why they protect all of us.

What the argument for retribution boils down to is often no more than a desire for vengeance masked as a principle of justice. The desire for vengeance can be understood and acknowledged, but the exercise of vengeance must be resisted. The history of the endeavor to establish the rule of law is a history of the progressive restriction of personal vengeance in public policy and legal codes.

If today's penal systems do not sanction the burning of an arsonists's home, the rape of a rapist, or the torture of a torturer, it is not because they tolerate the crimes. Instead, it is because societies understand that they must be built on a different set of values from those they condemn.

An execution cannot be used to condemn killing—it *is* killing. Whatever one's view of the retribution argument may be, the practice of the death penalty reveals that no criminal justice system is, or conceivably could be, capable of deciding fairly, consistently, and infallibly who should live and who should die.

KILLING THE INNOCENT

All criminal justice systems are vulnerable to discrimination and error. Expediency, discretionary decisions, and prevailing public opinion may influence the proceedings at every stage, from the initial arrest to the last-minute decision on clemency. The reality of the death penalty is that what determines who is executed and who is spared is often not only the nature of the crime but also the ethnic and social background, the financial means, or the political opinions of the defendant. The death penalty is used disproportionately against the poor, the powerless, the marginalized, or those whom repressive governments deem it expedient to eliminate.

Human uncertainty and arbitrary judgments are factors which affect all judicial decisions. But only one decision—the decision to execute—results in something that cannot be remedied or undone. Whether executions take place within hours of the trial or after years of appeals, states will continue to execute people who are later found to be innocent. Those executed cannot be compensated for loss of life, and the whole society must share responsibility for what has been done.

It is the irrevocable nature of the death penalty, the fact that the prisoner is eliminated forever, that makes the penalty so tempting to some states as a tool of repression. Thousands have been put to death under one government only to be recognized as innocent victims when another set of authorities comes to power. Only abolition can ensure that such political abuse of the death penalty will never occur.

When used to suppress political dissent, the death penalty is abhorrent. When invoked as a way to protect society from crime, it is illusory. Wherever used, it brutalizes those involved in the process and conveys to the public a sense that killing a defenseless prisoner is somehow acceptable. It may be used to try to bolster the authority of the state—or of those who govern in its name. But any such authority it confers is spurious. The penalty is a symbol of terror and, to that extent, a confession of weakness. It is always a violation of the most fundamental human rights.

Chapter Five

"DISAPPEARANCES"

When they tell you
I'm not a prisoner
don't believe them.
They'll have to admit it
some day.
When they tell you
they released me
don't believe them.
They'll have to admit
it's a lie
some day.

*Extract from "Last Will And Testament," by Ariel
Dorfman, from his book* Missing, *published by the
British Section of Amnesty International.*

On July 22, 1982, Saul Godinez Cruz "disappeared." At 6 A.M.
he mounted his motorcycle and rode off to work in Monjaras
de Chotuteca, Honduras. According to an eyewitness he was
stopped on the way by three men, one of them in military
uniform. They placed him and his motorcycle in a van with no
license plates. He was never seen again.

According to neighbors his house had been under obser-
vation, presumably by government agents, for some days
before his "disappearance."

In January 1989, the Inter-American Court of Human
Rights ruled that Saul Godinez Cruz was a victim of the human
rights abuse known as a "disappearance," and the government

of Honduras was responsible. The government has been ordered to pay his family compensation of $75,000.

The case was one of three considered by the court: in the case of Angel Velasquez, a "disappearance" was found to have occurred and compensation was awarded; in the case of Francisco Fairen Garbi, the court was not satisfied that the "disappearance" occurred in Honduras. These decisions were the first by any international tribunal on "disappearances" and have wide applications.

WHAT IS A "DISAPPEARANCE"?

A "disappearance" occurs when someone is apprehended and detained by a government or its security forces, but the detention is never acknowledged. The term was first used to describe abductions on a massive scale in Guatemala after 1966.

The practice goes back further. For example, the German High Command in occupied France issued the "Night and Fog" decree in 1942, under which everyone arrested for endangering German security was transferred from France to Germany under cover of night.

"Things are worse than I thought—now the Missing Persons Bureau has disappeared."
Nicholas Newman

The rationale for this was given by Field Marshal Keitel: "Intimidation can only be achieved by capital punishment or by measures by which the relatives of the criminal and the population do not know his fate."

Thirty years later, Night and Fog began to claim victims not only in Latin America but throughout the world, from India to Ethiopia, from the Philippines to Iraq. Between 1980 and 1988 the United Nations Working Group on Enforced and Involuntary Disappearances had investigated more than 15,000 cases in 40 countries.

"Disappearances," often followed by extra-judicial executions (sometimes called "political killings"), are on the increase. An extra-judicial execution is a deliberate killing carried out *by* government agents or *with* their complicity. This is different from the reasonable use of force to enforce the law, shooting in self-defense, or killings during armed conflict permitted under international law. Often, victims of extra-judicial executions are secretly abducted before being killed. The "disappearance" disguises the killing.

In its 1989 Annual Report, Amnesty International drew worldwide attention to a pattern of abuses in which thousands of people are killed each year by government agents acting beyond the limits of the law. It described the offenders and the victims in just one year, 1988:

> "The killing grounds are many and varied. Some alleged opponents of governments or people targeted because of their religion, ethnic group, language or political belief were killed in full public view; others in secret cells and remote camps. Some victims were shot down near apple fields, others in mosques and churches, hospital beds, public squares, and busy city streets. Prison cells and courtyards, police stations, military barracks, and government offices were all sites of political killings by agents of the state. But many people were killed in their own homes, some in front of their own families.
>
> "Victims were assassinated by snipers, blown up by explosive devices or gunned down in groups by assailants using automatic weapons. Others were stabbed,

strangled, hacked to death or poisoned. Many were tortured to death. In Columbia, Guatemala, El Salvador, Syria and the Philippines victims were often severely mutilated before they were killed. Their bodies were burned or slashed, ears and noses were severed and limbs amputated."

Sometimes victims are targeted because of their race: in Burundi the tension between the dominant Tutsi minority and the majority Hutu community led to the massacre of unarmed Hutus by Tutsi-dominated troops. Often a person's political opinion or trade union activity seems to be the reason they are "disappeared." In many countries it can be dangerous to speak out against "disappearances" and uphold human rights.

In the Philippines, for instance, Andrés Rio—journalist and Chairperson of the Human Rights Advocates of Leyte— was shot dead by soldiers from the 43rd Infantry Battalion. The soldiers claimed that he had been killed in an armed encounter, but local residents said he and others were arrested, burned with cigarettes and stabbed, before being shot dead by the soldiers. An investigation by a government body confirmed that the victims had not been killed in an armed encounter.

Armed conflict is often given as a reason for a "disappearance" or killing, as the 1989 Amnesty Report shows:

"A state of armed conflict was often the pretext as well as the context for government campaigns against those they considered undesirable. Warfare makes it easier to avoid accountability. Not only is access by independent civilians limited but the dead can be characterized as combatants killed in encounters or as the unavoidable civilian casualties of war....

"In Peru massacres and summary executions have largely replaced imprisonment and trial by the courts in counter-insurgency zones under the control of the military. In Sri Lanka both Sri Lankan and Indian troops have deliberately killed non-combatants in their efforts to suppress armed opposition groups. They were also responsible for 'disappearances'—secret unacknowledged arrests which result in execution."

Many "disappearances" take place in the context of violent opposition to a government. Amnesty International, as an organization working for human rights, condemns the violence and "disappearances" carried out by opposition groups. However, the organization addresses itself directly to the governments who are responsible for ensuring human rights in their country. All countries, as members of the United Nations, subscribe to the Universal Declaration of Human Rights and have a duty to protect the right to life, personal freedom, and humane treatment. In the case of Saul Godinez Cruz, the court found that these rights had been breached.

INVESTIGATING "DISAPPEARANCES"

It is not surprising that there have been no previous "disappearance" cases in international tribunals. "Disappearances" are shrouded in mystery. Those trying to collect evidence or obtain remedies are met with denials or intimidation.

In the Godinez case, two witnesses for the prosecution were killed by unidentified gunmen. One, the regional president of a human rights group, had just returned from giving evidence and was publicizing his testimony; the second, an army officer implicated in one of the abductions, was killed just before he was due to go to the court and give evidence. Other witnesses were threatened, and the court made a plea to the authorities to assure their safety.

Although governments are clearly accountable for the political prisoners they hold, they often deny responsibility for "disappearances," as the Honduran Government did in the Godinez case. Its defense consisted largely of undermining the credibility of witnesses by suggesting that they were politically motivated or unreliable because of their personal interest in the case, or disloyal because they were criticizing the government of Honduras. The government was criticized by the court for neglecting to provide evidence on the merits of the case.

The atmosphere in which any "disappearance" takes place means that any judicial investigation of the event is likely to meet with considerable obstruction. However, the Godinez case shows that these difficulties are not insurmountable. The court admitted evidence on the pattern of "disappearances" in Honduras between 1981 and 1984 from human rights groups, from a former army officer who was involved in the abductions, and from victims who had "disappeared" and been tortured but survived.

The court concluded that there was a pattern of "disappearances" which began when the victims, generally believed to be a danger to state security, were violently abducted by armed men in plain clothes using vehicles without license plates or with false license plates. The kidnap victims were then blindfolded, taken to secret detention sites, and often transferred from one site to another.

They were interrogated and subjected to harassment, cruel treatment, and torture. Some were killed and their bodies buried in clandestine cemeteries. The "disappearances" of 100–150 people in this way was usually attributable to the armed forces, who could rely on the tolerance of the government.

A common tactic used by authorities accused of human rights violations is to refer critics to a court procedure—which inevitably fails to uncover evidence of a violation or investigate it fully. The Honduran Bar Association put forward information about several remedies—from habeas corpus to civil and criminal cases—which are available to the families of the "disappeared" in Honduras. In fact, the family of Saul Godinez Cruz had put in three habeas corpus petitions and filed a criminal complaint, all to no avail.

The court noted that the petitions and the complaint had not obtained a result, and heard evidence of the intimidation of lawyers attempting to file habeas corpus petitions as well as the lack of success in producing the "disappeared" person. It concluded that the remedies available to the family in the country were not effective and stressed the responsibility of the state to investigate "disappearances" and to restore the victims' rights. The case shows both the difficulties of investigating the "disappearance" and the fruits of perseverance.

THE FAMILIES OF THE "DISAPPEARED"

The prolonged detention and isolation to which "disappearance" victims are subjected are themselves a violation of the right

GRIN & BEAR IT

Reprinted with special permission of North America Syndicate, Inc.

"My first act as president, after everyone is shot, will be to enact some meaningful human rights laws." **Fred Wagner**

to humane treatment, according to the Inter-American Court of Human Rights. This is quite apart from any other maltreatment which may occur during this time. Therefore "disappearances" can never be permitted under international human rights law.

In awarding compensation to the family of Saul Godinez Cruz, the court recognized the suffering of victims' families. Several studies on the families of the "disappeared" have identified three stages of response. At first, there is inaction due to fear of reprisals. This is followed by obsessive searching, with a high degree of anxiety. Meanwhile, the children of the "disappeared" suffer the psychological trauma of abandonment, loneliness, insecurity, and a permanent sense of fear.

There is a third stage of collective action and solidarity, exemplified by the Grandmothers of the Plaza de Mayo in Argentina who demonstrate regularly in central Buenos Aires, informing passers-by of the "disappearances" of their children and grandchildren during Argentina's "Dirty War" of the late 1970s and early 1980s. Their objective is at once simple and terribly complex—to shatter the shield of unreality, mystery, and disbelief surrounding "disappearances."

The family of Saul Godinez Cruz had refused the compensation set by the court on the grounds that money could not compensate for their loss, and that those responsible should be brought to justice. His mother said, "Our struggle is to see our family members alive, which would be our greatest satisfaction, or at least that they tell us where they killed and buried them. This is the uncertainty that tortures us and we want to see those responsible punished."

The report of the Godinez case is a remarkable document, for it is a story of courage: the courage of his family who refused to be intimidated into dropping the case, of the witnesses who testified while in fear of their own lives, of the lawyers who refused to let threats deter them from using the law to obtain justice, and of the "disappeared" who survived to give evidence.

WHAT AMNESTY CAN DO

However atrocious their behavior, governments do not like to be shamed in front of the world. By making their shabby human rights records public, Amnesty can help to make them accountable for "disappearances" and so help the families and even the victims themselves.

International public opinion, backed by human rights treaties, can make governments accountable for "disappearances," and shatter the mask of secrecy which they hide behind.

Publicity

Governments go to great lengths to conceal or destroy evidence of "disappearances," in order to avoid damaging publicity.

In Peru, a press exposé of an armed killing of 28 "disappeared" in the hamlet of Cayara in 1989 was followed by a government campaign to eliminate all evidence of the killing. The graves were dug up and the bodies moved. Local witnesses were killed, and access to the region by independent investigators was severely restricted.

It is important that the public is kept informed about such incidents, particularly because so many people have "disappeared" over the past 20 years. It appears that "disappearances" are being used by an increasing number of governments as a means of controlling and intimidating the opposition.

Amnesty International gives talks and screens films about "disappearances," and tries to publicize cases in the media both inside and outside the offending country. This publicity can generate powerful worldwide public demand for protecting the "disappeared" or for obtaining justice for their families.

Amnesty also helps to channel information on "disappearances" to international bodies. It is one of several human rights organizations which submit reports on "disappearances" in a number of different countries to the United Nations, the Inter-American Commission on Human Rights, the Organization of American States, and other human rights bodies. This promotes discussion on the international law concerning "disappearances," and increases the scope of influence that can be brought to bear on the offending country.

Relief

The families of the "disappeared" suffer through the uncertainty, the intimidation, and the secrecy surrounding "disappearances." Amnesty International helps by providing international support—moral, legal, and financial—to relatives of those who have "disappeared."

Urgent Action for the "disappeared"

Amnesty's Urgent Action Network is activated when it appears that the life or physical well-being of a prisoner is in danger, or he or she is under threat of execution or in serious ill-health due to poor prison conditions.

The UA Network is quick to respond to cases of "disappearances," for experience has shown that a person who has "disappeared" may often be killed or seriously tortured within the first few days of custody.

Amnesty advises members around the world to immediately send telegrams or letters, telexes, or faxes to the appropriate authorities asking that the death penalty be commuted, the torture stopped, or the prisoner receive immediate medical treatment.

You can join the Urgent Action Network by writing to Amnesty International. For more information, see page 119.

Chapter Six
RIGHTS OF
THE CHILD

Natalia Garcia, a Chilean girl aged 16 months, was imprisoned with her mother in a cell close to the one where her father was held. Both parents were tortured and could hear each other's cries. The child lacked proper food and care; her mother was unable to attend even to her most basic needs.

A report of Natalia's case by the *Vicaria de la Solidaridad,* a church human rights organization in Santiago, stated that the mental traumas produced were of such severity that the child rejected her mother and suffered psychological disturbances so serious that her mental health was permanently damaged. A signed medical certificate stated that "The CNI (Central Nacional de Informaciones) returned a little girl, frightened, nervous, who can't sleep, with marks and blotches all over her body.... The nervous condition of the little girl is without doubt very serious, and this is indicated by her insecurity and her fear of any person who approaches her."

"I have seen the Johnny referred to .... He spoke with great difficulty, as if his tongue was swollen and filled his mouth. He had a kind of lisp as well. His eyes were dull, as of someone who seemed to be dead to the world for much of the time. When he walked it was with a slow painful shuffle like a punchdrunk ex-boxer.

"And when I saw him I wanted to cry, but most all I was filled with a blazing anger against a system that could do this to a child in the bloom of youth who had all his life in front of him."

Bishop Desmond Tutu, on visiting Johnny Mashiane 16 months after his release from custody in South Africa

"Detention as such can permanently distort and deform a child's personality... it is aggravated by the failure to offer them an elementary level of protection while in custody...."

Swedish Children's Organization, Radda Barnen International, in a submission to the UN Commission on Human Rights

"In spite of all our follies and bitter failures across the wreckage of a broken world, may we strive and strive and never cease from striving till we have swept away the appalling blot which disgraces our civilization, this iniquitous child suffering."

Eglantyne Jebb, founder of Save the Children Fund

CHILDREN—A SPECIAL CATEGORY OF VICTIM

In over 50 countries, children have been detained without trial and imprisoned, tortured, and executed, solely for their non-violent expression of their beliefs or origins. Some are held in reprisal for the activities of adults; others suffer physical or mental torture designed to force family members to confess or give themselves up. Children have been forcibly adopted by strangers, brutalized to attempt to break their resistance, and even executed by their governments.

Amnesty International recognizes that children and young people are victims of political repression in ways specifically related to their age and social status, and they may be particularly targeted because of this.

Children are sometimes used as hostages or are tortured to force a relative to surrender, give information, or make a confession. Susana Tzoc Mendoza, a 13-year-old Guatemalan, was beaten with rifle butts over a four-day period in November 1988, by soldiers looking for her father, a human rights activist.

Similarly, the children of torture victims suffer greatly. "If a woman is tortured, then her whole family is tortured, even though they are not detained," said Mrs. Farkhandar Bhukari, a former political prisoner from Pakistan.

In some countries children have been taken from "subversive" parents and illegally adopted. There may be as many as 400 children missing in Argentina today as the result of a deliberate policy of forced adoption practiced during the late 1970s. Children of parents who "disappeared" at the hands of the security forces were either taken by families connected with those forces or sent to orphanages. Sra. Estela Carlotto was a founding member of the Grandmothers of Plaza de Mayo, a human rights group formed to trace the whereabouts of these "disappeared" children. Her own daughter, Laura, was a victim of Argentina's "dirty war." Pregnant when abducted on November 26, 1977, Laura is known to have given birth to a boy on June 25 or 26, 1978. Sra. Carlotto had the dead body of her daughter returned to her two months later, but never received any news of what had happened to her grandson. As she says:

> "Someone has him. Someone is bringing him up. Someone took him from my daughter five hours after he was born."

Many children have "disappeared" together with their families, or even with an entire community. In August 1983, 8,000 members of the Kurdish Barzani community were seized in Iraq. Among them were 315 children between 8 and 17 years of age at the time of their arrest. Their fate and whereabouts remain unknown.

Some children and young people are regarded as potentially "subversive" in their own right, and are subjected to detention and torture. Turkish schoolgirl Safinaz Ilboga was arrested at the age of 17 on a charge of "separatist propaganda" after she admitted that she was Kurdish to a teacher at her school who had said all Kurds were dirty and immoral. Arrested on the strength of information given to police by the teacher, she was held in prison for three weeks before her trial, and faced a maximum sentence of 15 years in jail if convicted.

Detention and ill-treatment of children on a large scale have recently been occurring in the territories occupied by Israel. In January 1990, Amnesty International reported that in the previous two years Israeli forces had shot and killed 130 children 16 years old and younger, 35 of whom were under 12. In South Africa more than 9,000 children, some as young as seven, were arrested between June 1986 and June 1989. Most had been assaulted in detention.

Many children imprisoned with their mothers often remain there for years, and some have never lived outside prison. Amonsissa Issa, an Ethiopian eight-year-old, has been in prison all his life. His mother, Namat Issa, a senior civil servant in the Ministry of Foreign Affairs, was arrested in February 1980, along with several hundred people of Oromo ethnic origin. No official reason was given for her arrest.

Amonsissa was held with his mother in the women's section of the Central Prison in Addis Ababa. In 1983, he caught a virus infection, possibly cerebral meningitis, and became seriously ill. He suffered brain damage and is now mentally disabled.

His case was highlighted by Amnesty's Youth Officer on a British children's television program, *Going Live,* on Human Rights Day, December 10, 1988. As a result, thousands of children sent him cards and gifts. Despite the initial refusal by the Ministry of Foreign Affairs in Addis Ababa to acknowledge Amonsissa's existence, the cards were successfully delivered. He was released with his mother during an amnesty in June 1989.

Children whose parents' lives are under threat and who, therefore, live in an atmosphere of violence and danger may inadvertently become casualties too. José Estuardo Sotz Alvarez, a Guatemalan seven-year-old, has been paralyzed from the waist down since May 1986, when his spinal cord was shattered by a bullet apparently intended for his father, a Guatemalan trade union leader. In 1989, Amnesty International sponsored the child's flight to Boston to undergo medical treatment at the Floating Hospital for Infants and Children. Physicians for Human Rights arranged for José's treatment at the hospital. Though paralyzed for life, today he is able to "walk" short distances with the aid of a walker.

Because of his trade union activities and the publicity given to his son's case abroad, José's father has apparently been blacklisted and has not been able to find work. With no income, he has had difficulty obtaining medical treatment for his son.

WORK TO HELP CHILD VICTIMS

Since their formation in 1977, the Grandmothers of the Plaza de Mayo have built up a large informal network which provides information on any suspicious adoptions, or children suddenly appearing in orphanages in Argentina. They are still trying to uncover exactly what went on during the years when the armed forces not only forcibly abducted, "disappeared," and killed thousands of adults, but also deprived hundreds of children of their real families.

One of the breakthroughs made by the Grandmothers, in association with the New York Blood Center and the American Academy for the Advancement of Science, is the ability to establish genetic identity with 98 to 99 percent certainty from blood samples taken from the child and from grandparents or aunts and uncles. Once the child's blood family has been identified, the next step in the process is perhaps the most delicate. The judge and a social worker have to tell the child who her or his family is, and what has happened. Although this is an enormous shock, the children soon accept what they have been told, and those who have so far been returned to their relatives have almost immediately shown improvements in their health and mental well-being.

In the Philippines, Dr. Elizabeth Protacio Marcelino, Professor of Psychology, runs a Children's Rehabilitation Center which she set up in 1985 to care for the children of political detainees who had been traumatized by their parents' suffering. Arrested herself under the Marcos régime, Dr. Marcelino was shocked to see how emaciated, fearful, damaged, and sick children became in prison as a result of the threats, brutal treatment, and constant interrogations they encountered.

Staff at the Children's Rehabilitation Center work intensely with some 300 children annually and maintain contact with another 1,200. These children have been politically im-

By permission of Mike Luckovich and Creators Syndicate

Mike Luckovich

prisoned with members of their family, many have been tortured, and some have spent their entire lives behind bars.

The Center uses puppets, theater, play, art, and stories to develop a therapeutic atmosphere and to help the children come to terms with their trauma. Together, the children begin to open up to each other about what they have been through. Other rehabilitation centers for such children in the Gaza Strip, Mozambique, South Africa, and Denmark provide similar vital support.

For the past few years the AIUSA Campaign Office in San Francisco has coordinated regular appeals and actions on behalf of children who are subject to arbitrary arrest, torture, execution, and "disappearance." Previous mailings have focused on selected Urgent Actions, cases from Amnesty International Week campaigns, appeals on behalf of street children in Brazil and Guatemala, and requests to urge ratification of the United Nations Convention on the Rights of the Child. On a regular basis, group members organize vigils, consular visits, art contests, and speaking engagements on a wide range of campuses.

RIGHTS OF THE CHILD—A NEW CONVENTION

Fortunately, the protection of child prisoners of conscience, and child victims of human rights abuses generally, has been greatly strengthened by recent international legislation focusing on children, particularly the adoption by the United Nations of the Convention on the Rights of the Child.

Broadly speaking, the Convention on the Rights of the Child, which defines a child as every human being under the age of 18, unless under the national law applicable to that child majority is attained earlier, is concerned with the four "P"s—prevention, protection, provision, and participation. It is concerned with developing preventive health care, eliminating child abduction, and prohibiting all unjustifiable discrimination against children. It aims at protecting children against all forms of torture, cruel, inhuman, and degrading treatment and punishment, abuse, and exploitation. Also, for the first time in binding international law, it entitles disabled children to participate fully in community life. The Convention also places a duty on states to provide rehabilitation for children who are victims of a wide range of abuses and neglect, and provides for equal access of all children to participation in cultural, artistic, and recreational activities.

International law has not yet reached the stage where the imprisonment of children is prohibited *per se*, but there is a definite trend toward limiting the imprisonment of children and minimizing the period of time for which a child can be deprived of liberty. The United Nations High Commissioner for Refugees has adopted guidelines on refugee children which specifically state that, due to their special situation, child refugees should not be detained. The Convention on the Rights of the Child strengthens the trend by establishing that children should only be arrested, detained, or imprisoned as a measure of last resort, and then only for the shortest appropriate period of time.

The Convention on the Rights of the Child has the potential to improve the lives of children worldwide. Firstly, it places a duty on governments to make the Convention widely known, not only to adults but also to children, in active ways that can be understood by both. Children will thus become aware of their rights, the first step toward protection.

Secondly, the Convention should have an impact on children's lives because it will establish an independent committee made up of experts on children's rights, which will receive regular reports from states on how each of the rights of the child are protected in their own countries. With the adoption of this Convenant, Amnesty International's work on behalf of children has been greatly strengthened.

In September 1990, Amnesty called all governments to stop the illegal killing, torture, and arbitrary imprisonment of children. AI issued the call in advance of the World Summit for Children, the largest gathering of world leaders ever, in New York that year.

"All too often children are victimized simply because of where they live or who their parents are," the appeal said. "Sometimes their age alone makes them targets for abuse. Children are often deliberately targeted for human rights violations because they are seen as a social or political threat."

In Brazil and Guatemala, where the number of street children has grown dramatically in recent years, children risk their lives simply by being on the streets. They are frequently tortured and extra-judicially executed by police on duty or in "death squads," often in the name of "cleaning up the streets."

In community raids in Peru's emergency zones, the military have singled out young people as a group, suspecting even those not involved in armed conflict of supporting the opposition. Frequently they are treated as pawns to get their parents to turn themselves in or to make confessions. In Iraq, children have been jailed and beaten, and many have disappeared.

"Of all the victims of human rights violations, children are the least able to stand up for their rights," said Amnesty's appeal. "Governments must, therefore, be particularly vigilant in protecting those rights."

Chapter Seven
CAMPAIGN FOR WOMEN'S RIGHTS

In 1986, a Moroccan court handed 34-year-old Nezha Al Bernoussi a six-year prison sentence. The woman's crime was officially described as "conspiracy against the security of the state, membership in an illegal organization, and distribution of unauthorized leaflets."

She believes the real reason for her imprisonment was her work on behalf of women's human rights in Morocco.

"I was committed to the struggle for the liberation of women in Morocco," she wrote in 1987 from her prison cell. "Before my arrest I gave courses in reading and writing for illiterate women of all ages. These courses were intended to teach women reading and writing on the one hand; on the other, the courses were intended to awaken their sense for scientific progress."

She remains in prison as of this writing.

The struggle for women's rights has frequently coincided with the struggle for human rights, and women have traditionally been in the front lines in both.

In the late 1970s and early 1980s, a small group of Argentine women stood virtually alone in challenging the military government. This small band of kerchiefed women first appeared in April 1977 at the height of what would later become known as Argentina's "Dirty War," a government-directed terror campaign against perceived subversives. Thousands of people were arrested, tortured, and subsequently "disappeared" between 1977 and 1983 during this campaign.

The generals derisively referred to the women as "Los locas de la Plaza de Mayo"—the crazy women of the Plaza.

Every Thursday they gathered in the square across from the Casa Rosada, the seat of Argentina's military government. Their protests were silent. Each woman carried a placard containing a photograph of a "disappeared" husband, son, or daughter and a simple question directed to their government: *Dondé Están?* Where are they?

Their silent vigil was a direct challenge to the military authorities behind the shuttered windows. One of the founders of the group, Azucena de Vinceti, was herself subsequently abducted and taken to the secret Navy Detention Center in the capital. She was never seen again.

In March 1990, Amnesty International launched the organization's first international campaign to end the abuse of women's human rights by governments. As part of that campaign the organization called on all world governments to implement a 12-point program to protect women from human rights violations.

"The international community can play a decisive role in protecting human rights through vigilant and concerted action," said Amnesty in announcing the campaign. "Governments that fail to protect fundamental human rights should be confronted with the force of international public opinion."

Women's human rights, like those of men and children, are proclaimed in the Universal Declaration of Human Rights. While both women and men all over the world continue to suffer the full range of human rights abuses, however, Amnesty International has long monitored a range of human rights violations that are primarily suffered by women.

Rape is one of them. Frequently used as a form of torture, it is most often inflicted on women detainees between the time of their arrest and arrival at an official detention center.

Maria Juana Medina was arrested by Salvadoran authorities in September 1989 at a union-sponsored demonstration. She was taken to the local police station, along with 63 other protesters. The police stamped her forehead for identification. Later she was summoned for interrogation.

"When my turn came to be interrogated, I was taken to a room," she said. "A man took off my clothes and began to question me. He made me lie on the floor and told me to take off my underwear. I said no. He took them off . . . ." They raped and beat her.

In Peru, rape by soldiers operating within specially designated counter-insurgency "emergency zones" has become so common that Peruvian officials told an Amnesty investigating team visiting the country in 1986 that rape "was to be expected" in rural areas, and that prosecutions for such assaults should not be anticipated.

A woman teacher who was detained for several days at a small army post in Abancay Department, Peru, alleged that she was stripped naked, suspended from a rope, slashed with a knife, and repeatedly raped. She was only released after school officials pressed for her release. She was threatened that she would be killed if she told anyone of her treatment in detention.

Rape sometimes appears to be used as a form of torture because those responsible realize their victims may be constrained from revealing what has occurred after their release from custody. The shame of rape can be a strong inducement to silence, and the victim's suffering can endure for the rest of her life.

But the sexual abuse of women in prison can take forms other than rape: verbal humiliation, forced acts of degradation, and strip searches are all common forms of intimidation practiced against women in all parts of the world.

Pregnant women face additional horrors during arrest and detention, including risk of injury to the fetus, miscarriage, and the risk of giving birth in harsh prison surroundings. Women who become pregnant in prison as a result of rape by prison guards face yet another trauma.

Patricia Pena, a 19-year-old Chilean woman, was arrested in September 1986 at a student demonstration. She was finally released on bail in 1988 and has since testified that she was tortured with an electric shock baton and raped in the initial hours after her arrest.

It was while Pena was serving her prison term that she realized she had become pregnant as a result of the rape. She began to experience severe pains and bleeding. Despite this she was denied medical treatment until she miscarried in late November 1986.

Threats of rape have been widely reported by women held in Turkish police stations. Police officers have reportedly

Drawing by Dana Fradon; © 1983 The New Yorker Magazine, Inc.

"How come you always take Amnesty International's side?"

Dana Fradon

stripped women detainees, sometimes in the presence of their relatives and associates, and tortured them. Solmaz Karabulut, who was arrested in March 1989 at the school where she taught, said police officers in Ankara accused her of belonging to an illegal organization, stripped her naked, threatened her with rape, and tortured her with electric shocks.

Misuse of prison regulations can also constitute cruel or degrading treatment. Strip-searching, conducted with the deliberate intention of humiliating the prisoner, is one example of such abuse. During 1986, guards at the Brixton Prison in England strip-searched two women prisoners virtually every day and sometimes up to three times daily. Amnesty International received allegations that these strip searches were a deliberate attempt to humiliate the women.

While it is frequently women working in community organizations or in fields where they may be perceived as threatening to the government—journalists, lawyers, women's rights activists, trade unionists, physicians, or teachers—who become targets of human rights abuses, women who are not politically active are not immune to abuse.

Merely being related to someone under suspicion can be enough to place a woman in peril. Wives, daughters, mothers, or friends of people considered subversive routinely become targets of abuse.

For many years Amnesty International has compiled documentary evidence of women being held as surrogates for relatives being sought by the authorities. Even though these women may themselves have done nothing, they are often tortured or killed in order to get at someone else. But even when women are not the direct object of government abuse, they frequently become indirect victims.

"We sit in our home day after day wondering what is happening to our children who are in prison," June Mlangeni, representing the Federation of Transvaal Women in South Africa, stated at a press conference in December 1987. She continued, "The effect of this type of worry causes the worst heartbreak any person can endure."

The wife of a Guatemalan trade unionist knows nothing of her husband's fate nine years after his "disappearance."

A two-year-old Guatemalan child and his mother were surrounded by four armed men in July, 1989. The men held guns to the child's head and threatened to kill him if his mother, Ana Graciela del Valle, failed to deliver a warning to her brother-in-law, the director of a Guatemalan human rights group.

Women whose husbands have "disappeared" endure in a kind of limbo in which, though they are effectively widowed, they are unable to claim state or other benefits because their husbands have never been declared officially or legally dead.

Members of the National Coordinating Committee of Widows of Guatemala, a non-governmental indigenous peoples human rights group, have documented their own government's attitude toward providing compensation to widows. The group charges that government compensation is granted only if a widow attributes her husband's death to opposition guerilla forces and only if she agrees to end investigations into his death.

Left alone to feed and protect their families, many women join the swelling ranks of the world's refugee population. The United Nations High Commissioner for Refugees has estimated that population is now more than 15 million. Most are women.

"Rape, abduction, sexual harassment, physical violence, and the not infrequent obligation to grant 'sexual favors' in return for documentation and/or relief goods remains a distressing reality for many women refugees," stated a legal advisor to the UN High Commissioner for Refugees in an article published in 1988.

In unfamiliar territory where they may not know the language or customs, these women lack the support systems which would be provided by their own families or communities.

Cultural or social circumstances sometimes also serve to isolate women. They may choose not to report humiliating assaults, fearing reprisals from their own families or the traumatic social repercussions that rape or sexual abuse may cause in some communities.

But the many women who do choose to speak out form the vanguard of a vast women's and human rights movement. Despite intimidation, these women continue to organize to demand human rights in every corner of the world.

In South Africa women carry much of the struggle for human rights.

Noma India Mfeketo is one of them. In 1985 she attended the United Nations International Women's Congress in Nairobi, Kenya as the representative of the United Women's Congress and the Federation of South African Women.

Her international prominence did not protect her when she returned home, however. In 1987 she spent nine months in detention without charge or trial and was again detained for several months in 1988 and 1989. Like many of her colleagues, she was detained solely for the peaceful exercise of her basic human rights.

Susan Aniban, leader of the Task Force Detainees, a human rights group in the Philippines, was detained and tortured in November 1988.

Turkish officials detained several members of a women's organization in January 1990 after police raided the offices of the Association of Democratic Women in Ankara. The women were reportedly tortured during interrogation.

Amnesty International's campaign to protect women's human rights will continue in the United States until the end of 1991. The campaign is being waged on the same fronts and the same issues as those to protect everyone's human rights, with a special focus on those abuses suffered primarily by women. The 12-point program that Amnesty International issued in conjunction with the campaign address these issues.

By focusing on human rights violations against women, AI hopes to mobilize international support for the protection of women and, by extension, for all members of society. When governments ignore their responsibility to one sector of society, no one's human rights are safe.

The following points form the basis of the campaign. Amnesty International believes they are essential to protecting the human rights of all women.

1. Stop rape and other torture and ill-treatment by government agents. Take effective steps to prevent rape, sexual abuse, and other torture and ill treatment of prisoners and detainees.

2. Stop persecution based on family connections.

3. Provide adequate health care to all detainees and prisoners. Provide all necessary prenatal and postnatal care to women detainees and their families.

4. Release all prisoners of conscience immediately and unconditionally.

5. Ensure prompt and fair trials for all political prisoners and detainees.

6. Take effective steps to investigate and prevent "disappearances."

7. Safeguard women's human rights in situations of armed conflict.

8. Prevent human rights violations against women refugees and asylum seekers. No woman, or any other asylum seeker, should be forcibly returned to a country where she can reasonably be expected to be imprisoned as a prisoner of conscience, tortured, or executed.

9. Prevent human rights violations against women who are members of ethnic minorities.

10. Stop judicial and extra-judicial executions and abolish the death penalty.

11. Ratify international instruments for the protection of human rights.

12. Support the work of relevant intergovernmental organizations.

CAMPAIGN GOALS AND STRATEGIES

Amnesty International's Campaign for women has three main objectives: educating Amnesty International members and the general public about the gender-specific violations experienced by women, pressuring world governments to observe international standards that protect the rights of women in custody, and working with other domestic organizations concerned with women's human rights to urge the United States Government to ratify the United Nations Convention on the Elimination of All Forms of Discrimination against Women.

A variety of strategies will be employed during the campaign. A series of seminars, workshops, and concerts around the country will focus on human rights abuses suffered by women. Amnesty International has also released a special report, *Women in The Front Line,* in conjunction with the campaign. Copies of the report are available from AIUSA's Publications Department.

Of course, a massive letter writing action on behalf of individual women who have experienced these abuses will be a prominent feature of the campaign.

Chapter Eight
FAIR AND PROMPT TRIALS

Mr. Lawman Mr. Lawman
May I speak with you
I'm a bit confused sir
what the law says I must do.
I know, many go to jail, sir
Because of the wrong they have done
But how many have been sent because they
are children of the sun.

Today in court sir
You lie and cheat on me
You know if you're found out sir
It could be perjury.
Mr Lawman don't be angry.
You know what I say is true.
Oh! Oh! Folks I'm off to jail
I'll be seeing you!!

Sidney Campbell, Jamaican ex-policeman
who was hanged on 16 March 1982

"Every day I receive a list of assassinations, threats, attacks and 'disappearances' .... I ask myself, What is this? This isn't democracy, this isn't a country. This is the law of the jungle."

Colombian Procurator General in a statement
to the press on 25 November 1987. Just two
months later he was abducted and murdered

"We're in trouble."   **Mick Stevens**

HUMAN RIGHTS AND THE LAW

Political prisoners in many countries are convicted in trials that violate internationally agreed standards, or are held for years, sometimes decades, without any trial at all. Amnesty International strives to ensure that *all* political prisoners are given a fair trial within a reasonable period of time, not just prisoners of conscience, whose release is sought regardless of criminal proceedings. While the term "prisoner of conscience" is strictly defined, the term "political prisoner" applies to any one who is imprisoned where there is a political element in the case. When political prisoners (suspected members of opposition groups that use violence, for instance) are not necessarily prisoners of conscience, AI urges that they be given a fair trial within a reasonable period, or, if charges are not brought, released.

AI bases its work for fair trials in such cases on internationally recognized standards that require:

— the provision of defense lawyers of the prisoner's choosing;

— full prior consultation with defense counsel;

— open trial in the presence of outside observers;

— the testimony of defense witnesses and right of cross-examination;

— the repudiation of evidence extracted under duress or torture.

In situations where administrative detention is used AI goes beyond work on behalf of individuals and presses for a general amnesty for all political detainees (if prisoners of conscience would benefit), for measures to ensure fair and prompt trials for detainees, or for repeal of the legislation under which they are held. Situations involving mass detention without trial are often the subject of AI reports.

Where trial procedures are notoriously unjust, as in military courts that try and sentence civilians who have no right of appeal or when the defendant is denied free access to legal counsel, or when the legislation under which prisoners of conscience are detained is itself a violation of the Universal Declaration of Human Rights, AI highlights this in its reports as well as in representations to the governments concerned.

In its work for fair trials AI may send lawyers from other countries to observe and assess political trials. In some instances cases of political prisoners convicted after unfair trials are assigned to AI groups for investigation as are cases of prisoners detained for long periods without trial.

When prisoners of conscience or individuals who are likely to become prisoners of conscience have difficulty obtaining the assistance of competent lawyers, AI looks into the possibility of providing legal aid. In countries where this is a problem on a large scale, AI may discuss the entire question of legal aid with the government and with appropriate bodies in the country, such as bar associations.

TRIAL OBSERVATION

From the earliest days of its work, Amnesty International has monitored political trials where there is likely to be unfairness, and where human rights may be at risk. To do this it relies

"Have you anything to say before you are found guilty?"

Len Spencer

upon independent observers: international legal professionals who are sent into the country in question to sit in on trial proceedings. An observer will, in every case, be familiar with AI and human rights work. All such international observers provide their services free of charge, while AI funds their travel and expenses.

Over the years that AI and other groups have sent observers to trials, a great deal of experience has been acquired, and much learned about the ways in which trial procedures can be distorted or used to the disadvantage of the defendant. Of course, each case must be considered on its own merits, but patterns of "unfairness" can be recognized, and in some cases international bodies such as the United Nations or the European Commission of Human Rights have criticized trials for blatant unfairness.

PROMPT TRIAL

Many people accused of crimes—real or concocted—endure months or years in prison before being brought to trial. Legal authorities are generally expected to bring someone to trial within a "reasonable" time. What is reasonable depends, of course, on a variety of factors, including the complexity of the case, the accused person's own conduct, and the way in which the case is handled by the judicial authorities.

A trial may also be unfair, even if the delay is not for such a long period, if that delay hampers the ability of the accused person to defend him or herself, for instance by allowing evidence to be destroyed. Fundamental to the gathering of evidence for any trial is the principle that it should be obtained as soon as possible after the event or crime to which it relates. To deny this opportunity to a defendant is, in some cases, to deny him or her justice. In addition, the delays in hearing appeals of court decisions can impose enormous psychological burdens on prisoners who are already suffering—particularly if they are appealing against a death sentence.

UNFAIR LAWS

The variety of laws which result in the violation of human rights is enormous. There are certain elements of any law which determine whether or not it is likely to be fair and just. One element which is essential is fairness. Laws must not discriminate. This principle is stated quite simply by the Universal Declaration of Human Rights:

> "All are equal before the law and are entitled without any discrimination to equal protection of the law."

Therefore, any law which gives greater protection or more rights to one sector of society over another is necessarily in breach of this basic right. It follows that if the laws being imposed are unfair, it is almost impossible for the trial itself to be fair.

Another factor essential to the fairness of any law is that it must not be retroactive. This means that an activity which was legal at the time it occurred should not be made criminal

SUBURBAN COWGIRLS

Janet Alfieri and Ed Colley

by a later law. The reasons for this are clear—that people are entitled to know whether or not they are breaking the law at the time of their actions.

ACCESS TO LAWYERS

One of the essential rights to which all accused people are entitled is the right to put forward their own explanation of the events leading to the trial.

Depending on the legal system, this right may consist of the opportunity to put forward legal submissions; to argue against the prosecution's interpretation of a particular law; to call or cross-examine witnesses; or to put forward evidence in written form.

Essential to the exercise of this right is the entitlement of the accused person to be present during the trial or hearing. Any trial which takes place in the absence of the defendant, or where the defendant is not given the opportunity to be present, gives rise to doubts about its fairness.

Everybody who comes before a court of law in any country is likely to be at a disadvantage if he or she is not familiar with the procedure and rules of the court. For that reason, access to a lawyer and to legal advice is essential to the presentation of a case. When prisoners of conscience or individuals who are likely to become prisoners of conscience have difficulty obtaining the assistance of competent lawyers, AI looks into the possibility of providing legal aid. In countries where this is a problem on a large scale, AI may discuss the entire question of legal aid with the government and with appropriate bodies in the country, such as bar associations.

If a defendant is denied access to legal advice or to legal representation, the presentation of a proper defense can be almost impossible. In cases of denial of access to a lawyer, groups of AI lawyers send appeals, publicize cases in legal journals, and activate national and international legal organizations to which they belong in an effort to ensure that prisoners receive the legal support to which they are entitled.

SENTENCE WITHOUT SAFEGUARDS

At least 37 countries have special or military courts empowered to pass death sentence without safeguards or without the right to appeal. Executions have been carried out within hours or even minutes of sentencing, leaving no time for those concerned to appeal or ask for clemency.

In Iran, thousands of political prisoners have been tried by Islamic Revolutionary courts where many of the normal safeguards do not exist. In the eleven years since the foundation of the Islamic Republic of Iran in 1979, Amnesty International does not know of one instance where a political prisoner facing the death penalty has been defended by a lawyer. In some cases a presumption of the guilt of the accused meant the trial lasted a matter of minutes and consisted only of reading out the charge and passing sentence.

EVIDENCE

The use of torture to extract confessions is common. AI has documented cases from countries around the world in which individuals facing trials have been convicted on the basis of their own confessions extracted under torture. Even when torture has not been used, there may still be circumstances of oppression, which means that confession of guilt is not reliable. The convictions of the Guildford Four in the UK—eventually overturned on appeal in 1989—were based largely on their own confessions which had been made and subsequently retracted. This problem is widely recognized in international legal circles and the United Nations Convention against Torture, which has been signed and ratified by a growing number of governments, prohibits the use of torture and the use of "evidence" in court obtained by the use of torture.

It goes without saying that the use of such evidence will render a trial unfair.

JUDGES

While an honest and independent judge may compensate for other unfair aspects of a case, a judge who is partial or biased will almost inevitably render a trial unfair and unjust. It may be very difficult to assess the intentions of a judge, but it is generally easier to determine his or her independence.

Judges who are afraid of losing their job are less likely to make decisions which might upset their government. Security of tenure, therefore, is generally regarded as essential to true independence: judges should not be liable to dismissal except in cases of judicial incompetence or demonstrable unfitness (where they are shown to be behaving dishonestly).

In many countries, however, governments seek to influence judges by undermining their independence. Further, if a government fails to protect lawyers or judges from threats, such as those issued by death squads, the effect is the same as if the government were making the threats itself. This is a recurring problem in many countries, including Colombia where, in 1988, there were only six lawyers who would risk representing those charged for their activities in opposition groups. The campaign of violence and intimidation in Colombia had forced all others to be silent or to leave the country.

One human rights organization, known as the Center for the Independence of Judges and Lawyers (CIJL), specializes in the study of this field and operates from Geneva, having been established under the aegis of the International Commission of Jurists. The center has documented cases from all over the world of judges and lawyers facing threats to their impartiality, and of unfair trials which result from that.

PUBLIC ACCESS

The Universal Declaration of Human Rights states that everyone is entitled to a "fair and public" hearing in determining any charge brought against them.

The public image of secret trials may still be linked to the days of Stalinism in the USSR and the "midnight knock" by the secret police. But secret trials are a problem in many countries, and frequently the secrecy of a trial indicates that not only is it unfair, but also that the government is trying to cover up that fact.

In Eastern Europe many past trials supposedly held in public were effectively held in secret. Observers from AI and other human rights organizations were denied access to the trials, although the authorities claimed that the public gallery was full. Often these galleries were filled with police or government employees to ensure that there would not be room for independent observers who might report on the proceedings.

There are exceptions to the general rule that trials of criminal matters should always be held in public. Some provisions of international human rights conventions specifically allow for all or some of a trial to be held in camera if this is necessary to protect the individuals concerned.

Unfair trials have probably occurred in every country of the world, and have marred every legal system at some time. The vigilance of organizations such as AI is one guard against injustice, but only one. Justice can only be guaranteed by openness in conducting trial proceedings, an alert public, honesty and integrity on the part of judges, and the readiness of lawyers to act fearlessly on behalf of the individual on trial.

Chapter Nine
REFUGEES

WHO ARE ASYLUM SEEKERS?

"Everyone has the right to seek and to enjoy in other countries asylum from persecution." (Article 14, Universal Declaration of Human Rights, 1948)

Throughout the world, millions of men, women, and children are suffering from oppression and persecution on account of their race, religion, or beliefs. In order to escape imprisonment, torture, or execution, many have no alternative but to leave their homeland and seek refuge elsewhere—to become asylum seekers.

Oppression and persecution are not confined to any one region or political system. Asylum seekers include Tamils from Sri Lanka, Kurds from Turkey, government critics from China, Sudan, and Iraq, all at risk simply for exercising the rights that many people take for granted. When asylum seekers flee from their own country they leave behind their families and their livelihood, everything that is familiar; their lives are completely disrupted. For many the achievements of their education and employment may be lost, with relatively few opportunities available to them in the country of asylum.

When Chuy Medina woke up in a hospital in El Salvador, he learned he had been left for dead by agents of that country's military. Since he had heard that the police and military occasionally kidnapped persons out of hospital beds, he fled the hospital before his release and left his country for the United States, intending to join his sister in Chicago. He crossed the border in south Texas and was detained by the

Immigration and Naturalization Service. Released on bond, he subsequently traveled to Chicago from Texas, but failed to appear in Immigration Court. He was unaware of his rights and obligations because he had been given bad advice by a notary public in Chicago. When he failed to show, the INS issued an order for his deportation.

Each year thousands of people arrive in the United states seeking refuge from governmental repression. Too many of

Steve Bell

these people are sent back to a fate that almost certainly includes imprisonment, torture, or even execution. Medina's case was referred to AIUSA's refugee office by a local group member. An AI staff member interviewed him and became convinced of his truthfulness. His case was turned into an AI letter-writing action calling for his asylum claim to be reopened. As a result of this campaign, INS officials withdrew their opposition to reopening the claim, and the case was transferred to Chicago. The AI Refugee Office in San Francisco provided relevant AI reports on El Salvador to Chuy Medina's attorney, as well as an affidavit in support of his claim to the protection of the United States. AI group members and staff also attended his hearing before the Immigration Judge in Chicago. As a result of these efforts and superb work by a volunteer attorney, Chuy Medina was granted political asylum in the spring of 1989.

The growing number of refugees in the world, now some 15 million, is a continuing reminder of the need to fight human rights abuse. The refugee problem will not go away and cannot be ignored. Until human rights abuse is eradicated, people will continue attempting to cross borders, seeking freedom from the oppression they have every reason to fear.

AMNESTY'S WORK ON BEHALF OF REFUGEES

Amnesty has been involved in refugee work since its inception. The work and involvement has grown as the international refugee crisis has become a major human rights concern.

While AI is not primarily a refugee organization, it works to prevent persons from being forcibly returned to countries where they are likely to become prisoners of conscience or suffer torture or execution. The nature of AI's involvement reflects its special expertise in the documentation of human rights violations worldwide and its concerns about asylum seekers. Refugee work is the second exception to the prohibition against AI members being involved in human rights issues in their own countries.

The organization's practical contribution is often to demonstrate whether an individual asylum seeker's fears are justified, or "well founded." It does so by providing evidence of specific human rights abuses to the authorities and to the lawyers and organizations working on the individual's behalf.

Amnesty is able to put the request for asylum into its human rights context by using the information available to it through its research into the human rights violations that occur in so many parts of the world.

Amnesty will continue to work on behalf of refugees as long as human rights violations force people to leave their own countries. We must also continue to persuade the governments of countries where people seek asylum not to implement laws and practices which make it difficult for the victims of human rights abuse to leave their own countries and seek asylum in safe countries.

GOVERNMENTS' OBLIGATIONS TO ASYLUM SEEKERS

The spectacle of thousands of people leaving their own countries because of persecution is not a new one. Throughout history, war, religious persecution, and political upheaval have forced people to leave their homelands and seek asylum elsewhere. The twentieth century has seen huge movements of refugees fleeing persecution and the devastation of war. In 1956, the uprising in Hungary caused many refugees to flee to the West; another wave followed the 1968 Soviet invasion of Czechoslovakia. After the coup in Chile in 1973, many Chilean refugees sought sanctuary; and thousands of Indo-Chinese, displaced by the Vietnam War and conflict in Cambodia, have been resettled in the West. In the 1980s, massive repression in Guatemala and El Salvador and human rights abuse in Nicaragua caused thousands to seek safety in Central and North American countries.

Unfortunately, there is a growing tendency for governments to treat asylum applications as unfounded, or to suggest that asylum seekers' fears of persecution are exaggerated. Confronted by large numbers of people fleeing from persecution, some governments have reacted by trying to turn them away, rather than by trying to stop the persecution. Some governments have introduced measures that may actually prevent refugees from setting foot in their countries.

The result is that people fleeing state terror now increas-

"How do you explain the fact that whenever we like a government somewhere, the people there usually don't agree with us?"

J. B. Handelsman

ingly face a risk of being sent back to countries where they are in danger of being imprisoned as prisoners of conscience, tortured, or executed. That is, of course, if they are able to flee from their country of origin in the first place, despite the imposition of stringent visa requirements on nationals of refugee-producing countries and the fines imposed on airlines that carry passengers without proper documentation.

The granting of asylum to those in fear of persecution is not just an act of humanity—those nations who have signed the 1951 United Nations Convention Relating to the Status of Refugees are legally committed not to return refugees to countries where they are at a risk of persecution.

A refugee is defined as any person with a "well-founded fear of persecution for reasons of race, nationality, membership of a particular social group or political opinion," who is outside his or her country of origin and, due to such a fear, is "unwilling to return to it" (Article 1 of the 1951 UN Convention).

Governments must not expel or return a refugee "in any manner whatsoever" to a country where his or her "life or freedom would be threatened" (Article 33 of the 1951 UN Convention).

LEGISLATION TO PROTECT REFUGEES

Amnesty International presented its concerns and suggestions when Congress drafted and debated the 1980 Refugee Act. This important law incorporated language of the 1951 United Nations Convention Relating to the Status of Refugees. The 1980 Refugee Act amended the Immigration and Nationality Act of 1952, eliminating the geographical and ideological bias in favor of those fleeing Communist countries or the Middle East which that act contained. Anyone in the US, "irrespective of status," became eligible to apply for political asylum.

Since the passage of the Refugee Act, AI has monitored its implementation. AIUSA's Washington staff testified in Congress against the interdiction of Haitian refugees on the high seas and the discriminatory detention of certain groups of asylum seekers in the 1980s. AI has worked with other organizations in favor of legislation that provides better protection for refugees, and at times has mobilized its membership to advocate specific measures. AI testified before Congress in favor of the Moakley-DeConcini Bill, which would have given temporary protected status to Salvadorans (later, Nicaraguans were added to the bill). In letters and visits AI members expressed support for the bill to members of Congress, and campaigned in their communities to mobilize support. Salvadorans were finally granted "temporary protected status" (freedom from deportation for 18 months) through the Immigration Act of 1990.

Amnesty groups are urged to participate in legislative efforts to promote safeguards and protection for refugees facing "refoulement" (forcible return to their country of origin or another country where they may face danger). Letter-writing and visits to members of Congress are crucial elements of group work for the protection of refugees. These activities are initiated by the Refugee Office or the Washington office and are carried out with the help of the regional offices. Groups are informed of action requests through mailings from the Refugee Office, the Monthly Mailing, or other AI network mailings.

INDIVIDUAL ASYLUM CASES IN THE UNITED STATES

In order to receive political asylum, individuals must present their cases to the federal government and prove that they qualify. In most cases this is not easy. Refugees often flee their homes without having time to gather the necessary documents, such as evidence of death threats or newspaper articles naming them as subversive. Once they are here, many new arrivals face language and cultural problems that make the process of asylum application seem insurmountable. While AI does not have the means to provide direct legal assistance to all or even a substantial number of these people, it can help in several different ways.

Staff and members of the Legal Support Network can inform individuals of appropriate refugee agencies. AI local groups can survey their communities to become informed of which agencies offer legal and social services to various nationalities. Following training, AI members may work with such agencies, assisting them with documentation, visiting detention centers to interview refugees, and other work. All AI offices can provide general information to asylum seekers and their attorneys. If AI decides to support a claim, it can express its support in a letter to the immigration authorities, through letter-writing campaigns by members, by asking local group members to attend asylum hearings, by providing relief, and through other means.

The degree of involvement of each section in refugee work has varied according to the situation in each country. For most of the past ten years, the US section has focused on two areas: US refugee legislation and policy, and individual casework. The casework activity has primarily involved the providing of documentation of human rights abuses relevant to an asylum applicant's case.

"What happened to all those nice flags of the world?"

Henry Martin

Interested groups and members are urged to seek instruction from their regional office to become involved in the following refugee-related activities:

— By studying their communities to learn which agencies offer assistance to asylum seekers, what nationalities of asylum seekers live in their area, what Immigration & Naturalization Service District they are in, and where in their area asylum seekers are detained.

— By passing on information on asylum cases to the San Francisco Refugee Office for evaluation.

— By organizing campus and community presentations or events with refugee themes, both local and worldwide.

AI members should be careful to undertake information gathering from public officials in an objective manner. As noted above, contacts with public officials, including the INS, should be cleared with the regional office.

DETENTION IN US FACILITIES

AI does not oppose a government's right to detain individuals who enter a country without proper documentation. AI does, however, call on governments to demonstrate legitimate reasons for any detention of asylum seekers. Detention must be the result of a prompt, fair individual hearing before a judicial or other similar authority whose status and tenure afford the strongest possible guarantees of competence, impartiality, and independence. If these effective safeguards do not exist or are not followed, AI will oppose the practice of detention.

Though Amnesty guidelines specifically prohibit condemnation of prison conditions in one's own country, AI may oppose circumstances of detention or any other restrictive measure that, intentionally or not, obstructs individuals at risk of human rights abuse from gaining access to a country's refugee determination procedure. Information on such potential abuses is sent to the San Francisco office for action by AIUSA in consultation with the International Secretariat.

RESPONSES TO ASSISTANCE

The assistance Amnesty provides refugees is invaluable. The accuracy and impartiality of its research, and its reputation as a reliable source of information have helped many refugees to gain asylum. The following are letters written by some of the people involved:

> "The Immigration Judge's decision was based in large part on the information which you were able to send us. This is the first time of which I am aware that this Immigration Judge has granted asylum to a Salvadoran."
>
> *Lawyer who used AI reports*
> *to help win an asylum case*

"I am writing to thank you for all your support and assistance in an effort to gain the release of my brother... from an Iraqi... camp. He has been released and this could not happen without the help of people like you."

Relative of an Iranian refugee whose
brother's case was handled by the US and
Swedish sections of AI

"I firmly believe that... the supporting background documentation... was a very important consideration in the judge's opinion."

Attorney's comments regarding a Guatemalan
who obtained asylum

"Mr. Aziz, a Lebanese Palestinian, was granted suspension of deportation. (He) is extremely happy and asked me to write and express his gratitude."

Letter from immigration lawyer

"I want to thank you for sending [an AI group member] to us. Her presence at the hearing clearly affected the outcome, as the judge has great respect for Amnesty International's material."

Attorney representing an
Iranian asylum seeker

"It was a real pleasure to assist you folks by attending the asylum hearing at INS headquarters.... As I told some of my fellow Amnesty members, we are accustomed to reading reports on human rights cases... but the real essence of such agonizing instances only begins to appear when you listen to a firsthand account in great detail.

Letter to the Refugee Office from a group member
who attended an asylum hearing (Group 24)

"I have found that Amnesty International's position with respect to my clients has been very helpful...particularly...with Somalian political asylum claims."

Letter from an attorney representing several asylum applicants

"Thanks for your letter on Ricardo Mendoza. Your response to the BHRHA [State Department] letter has made all the difference in the world."

Attorney representing a Central American asylum applicant

Chapter Ten
HUMAN RIGHTS EDUCATION

"The study of human rights in schools should lead to an understanding of and sympathy for the concepts of justice, equality, freedom, peace, dignity, individual rights and democracy.

"The emphasis in teaching and learning about human rights should be positive.

"Throughout their school career all young people should learn about human rights as part of their preparation for life in a pluralistic democracy.... Concepts associated with human rights can and should be acquired from an early age....

"Schools are communities which can and should be an example of the respect for the dignity of the individual and for difference, for tolerance and for equality of opportunity."

Council of Europe, 1985

HUMAN RIGHTS EDUCATION AND THE UNITED NATIONS

On December 10, 1948, following the devastation of World War II and the emergence of the terrible truth about the Nazi period—"barbarous acts that have outraged the conscience of mankind"—the leaders of the world met at the United Nations and pledged to promote "universal respect for, and observance of, fundamental rights and freedom."

Education was seen as a major antidote to the abuses the world had just experienced. Citizens who understood their rights would surely struggle to uphold and develop them.

Each member nation was urged to teach its people all about this new charter, and the General Assembly required "every individual and every organ of society" to "strive by teaching and education to promote respect for these rights and freedoms." The Assembly spoke of "the inherent dignity and the inalienable rights of all members of the human family," and the protection of human rights as the "foundation of freedom, justice and peace in the world."

AMNESTY INTERNATIONAL—DEVELOPING HUMAN RIGHTS AWARENESS

Most of Amnesty International's activities are limited to concerns about the human rights of prisoners spelled out in the organization's mandate: the release of prisoners of conscience, an end to torture and executions, and fair and prompt trials for political prisoners. However, an important objective of Amnesty International has also been to help develop awareness of and respect for human rights around the world. In this educational work AI takes a much broader approach to human rights, seeking to widen public understanding about all 30 Articles in the Universal Declaration of Human Rights.

In 1988, to mark the 40th Anniversary of the Declaration, Amnesty International organized a world tour with top international rock musicians Bruce Springsteen, Sting, Tracy Chapman, Peter Gabriel, and Youssou N'Dour. The tour brought the human rights message to live audiences of over a million young people and to over a hundred million television viewers at concerts in more than 20 countries.

Most of Amnesty's human rights education work is not centrally initiated, but developed by the national sections in ways that are appropriate to their differing local situations, cultures, traditions, educational systems, languages, and priorities.

ADULT EDUCATION

This human rights education is not restricted to the young. The Dutch Section runs special human rights awareness courses for the business community, the police, and officials in the

PEOPLE ALL
OVER
THE WIDE
WORLD
UNITE AND
WITH
ONE
VOICE
DEMAND FREE
VERSE

K. Lamb

Kathryn Lamb

Foreign Ministry. The British Section has produced an excellent handbook and introductory course in human rights for use by trade unions. A number of Sections, including the one in Israel, have organized human rights education programs for the armed forces. The British Section has designed a 17-poster exhibition for adult education purposes, and this is widely used in libraries and community centers by local groups to explain the work of the organization. In 1991, AIUSA initiated a special program to educate the general public about women's rights as human rights. The program features public forums and speakers tours in all regions of the country.

The multiplicity of languages worldwide is a special challenge for the sections. For the 80,000 people of the Faroe Islands, the local Amnesty Section had to translate human rights and Amnesty texts from Danish into the local Faroese language to make them more accessible. In countries like

Papua New Guinea, Sierra Leone, and Bangladesh, where adult literacy is low, Amnesty human rights education sessions are often conducted using films and slide presentations, instead of relying on the written word.

AMNESTY AT WORK IN SCHOOLS

The bulk of Amnesty's human rights education work around the world is done in schools and colleges. Sections develop their own materials and approaches for use in schools, and offer training and conferences for teachers.

AIUSA has a National Steering Committee on human rights education which believes that teaching about human rights should be "The Fourth R"—and should occupy as central a place in the school curriculum as the traditional "Three Rs"— reading, writing, and arithmetic. The Steering Committee produces and distributes a quarterly newsletter called "The Fourth 'R'."

This human rights curriculum includes the study of civil and political rights, and of economic and social rights. Students learn about responsible citizenship, the rule of law, the history of the human rights movement over the centuries, and about their fundamental rights and freedoms. They learn about patterns of human rights abuse and about international understanding and democracy.

The way in which human rights are taught has increasingly moved from conventional "frontal learning" about the content of human rights texts to developing the skills necessary to work for human rights. Such skills grow out of active participation and experiential learning. AIUSA has developed a network of letter-writing groups for children aged from nine years old, who with the support of teachers or parents respond to monthly Amnesty Urgent Action appeals—often concerning young peoples' cases—that have been specially rewritten in easier language.

The Urgent Action office in Colorado offers a Special Children's Edition Urgent Action each month. A simplified UA casesheet is provided, accompanied by the original casesheet for the teacher. Teachers have incorporated human rights education into their curriculum using the children's Urgent

Actions in many ways. Many teachers have made letter writing a voluntary project, and children in some classes write letters to US officials about a number of domestic issues of concern. Others write letters on behalf of victims of governmental abuse to officials abroad, as suggested in the UAs. One teacher had the children in her class handle a PoC's case in debate form. Many teacher's find that the Universal Declaration of Human rights fits into almost any subject at any grade level.

EDUCATION PROJECTS

In some countries AI has developed ways of contributing to local and national education programs. Special materials prepared for schools include teaching kits on AI, and other educational materials including general literature and articles on human rights issues designed to stimulate discussion (such as a course on "Prison Literature"), and facts about human rights violations.

Some national AI sections have devised material and approaches for quite young children. The Italian Section has an educational program for primary schools, *Insieme Si Puo* (Together We Can), based around the witty story of the rise and fall of an outrageous tyrant called King Trucibaldi, rejected by his people because of his unjust laws.

In 1985, the Human Rights Education Working Group in the British Section of Amnesty, with the help of Professor Ian Lister, Head of the Education Department of York University, produced *Teaching and Learning about Human Rights.* This illustrated human rights education pack in 12 units was designed to assist classroom teachers who were beginning to introduce human rights into schools in the UK.

Amnesty has also produced educational videos on human rights. Many are for secondary school and college students, covering such topics as the death penalty, successful campaigns to free political prisoners, trade unionists' rights, and government repression, among others.

One video, *The Universal Declaration of Human Rights,* is a unique blend of talent from 41 international animators. Created in celebration of the 40th anniversary of the Universal Declaration of Human Rights, this animated video brings the

*"Maintaining confidence between the people and the government is
extremely important. Lately I, the government, have been losing
confidence in you, the people."* **J. B. Handelsman**

document's 30 articles to life in an entertaining and educational manner. It is available in Spanish, French and Arabic, as well
as in English.

In addition to its regular reports on abuses in specific
countries, Amnesty publishes a variety of books on human
rights. These include publications on torture, US refugee
policy, and anthologies of articles about and interviews with
people whose rights have been abused. Many other
workbooks, AIUSA documents, and materials are available in
a catalog provided by the organization. For more information
write to the Publications Unit at the AIUSA's office in New York
(see below for the address).

WHAT YOU CAN DO

In 1948 the General Assembly called on all member states to
publicize the text of the United Nations Declaration of Human
Rights, and to "cause it to be displayed, read and expounded

principally in schools and other educational institutions, without distinction based on the political status of countries." Through its work in the Educators Network, which reaches out to educators across the country, AIUSA seeks to respond to this call. If you would like to become involved in this aspect of Amnesty's work, please contact AIUSA, 322 Eighth Avenue, New York, NY 10001; (212) 807-8400.

Simon Bond

AMNESTY'S STRUCTURE, AND OPPORTUNITIES FOR ACTION

Chapter Eleven

THE STRUCTURE OF AMNESTY INTERNATIONAL

"Hello Amnesty International, I'm . . . from Karl-Marx-Stadt, German Democratic Republic. Amnesty International is a very sensible organization. I find it right that an organization stands up for human rights, an important matter in the world. I do not know enough about your organization. That is why I want material about Amnesty International. Please! Give me the possibility. Thank you."

This is one of the many letters which arrive every day at the International Secretariat of Amnesty International in London. They come from around the world, from women and men who simply want to do something about human rights for other people. Countless others contact their local Amnesty International offices.

In 1989, increasing numbers of people sent letters from Eastern Europe requesting information and asking to take part in Amnesty International's work. By the end of the year, over 200 people worldwide had become international members including, for the first time, people in Hungary, Poland, the island of Antigua in the Caribbean, Malaysia, the People's Republic of Mongolia, Taiwan, and Vietnam. In some of these countries international members began to form groups, meeting on a regular basis.

INTERNATIONAL STRUCTURE

Members in 45 countries are formally organized into sections. They elect and send representatives to the International Council Meeting (ICM) held every two years. As the supreme governing body of Amnesty International, the International Council interprets the mandate and determines policy. It elects eight members of the International Executive Committee (IEC), whose ninth member is a staff representative from the International Secretariat. The International Executive committee meets four times a year to supervise the work of Amnesty International. It hires the Secretary General, who directs the movement and is in charge of the staff of the International Secretariat.

The movement's center for the collection and dissemination of information is the International Secretariat in London. The Research Department, the Documentation Center, and the Legal Office monitor and report on the human rights situation worldwide. The Press and Publications and the Campaign and Membership Departments coordinate action in response to that research.

AMNESTY INTERNATIONAL USA

In the United States working members vote on policy at the Annual General Meeting and elect a Board of Directors, which meets five times a year to develop policy and oversee the work of Amnesty International USA. The Board hires the Executive Director, who with the Deputy Director represents AIUSA publicly and oversees the work of the section.

National Office

At the National Office in New York the staff is organized into three main areas of activity: programs, communications, and finance. The Executive Director is responsible for all the work of the section. A Senior Deputy Executive Director is in charge of the day-to-day operation of the organization. There are also individual Deputy Executive Directors for both Programs and Finance who coordinate the work of the section including administration, fundraising, membership activities, and program work.

The Communications Unit broadens public awareness and support of Amnesty International by establishing and maintaining contacts with the media, printing and distributing Amnesty International publications, coordinating major special events, and creating publicity literature and audiovisuals.

The section's contacts with the United States government are coordinated at the Washington, DC office, where staff with regional expertise advise both the organization and the government. The Washington office also arranges embassy visits.

Regional Offices

Regional offices in Boston, Atlanta, Chicago, and Los Angeles, with a second Western office in San Francisco, coordinate membership, campaign work, fundraising, and press activities in their regions. They work closely with area coordinators, student area coordinators, and experienced volunteer leaders responsible for AI group activity in a local area. They also help groups establish themselves and thrive. When in doubt about who can help solve a problem, members contact their regional office.

GROUPS

Since its inception in 1961, Amnesty International has depended on its groups to provide the inspiration and organization that make it possible for individuals all over the world to influence government policy. The group is the link between AI and the community, between AI and the individual prisoner. Most likely, if the group is inactive, the community remains silent and the prisoner helpless.

Around the world, groups of 10–25 people gather every few weeks to curb the killing, stop the torture, and get prisoners of conscience out of jail. Local and student Amnesty International groups involve their communities in campaigns and prisoner work. They write letters, publicize human rights concerns, plan educational and fundraising events, and approach other groups, such as labor unions, journalists, religious organizations, and government representatives to involve them in human rights work. Because of the strength of their commitment, they are able to convince large numbers of people to take action to protect the human rights of strangers halfway across the globe. There are over 400 groups in the US, working on behalf of victims of human rights abuses.

Why do people join local groups? One new member stressed "the chance to meet with, and get to know, people who share similar opinions ... but most importantly, it is a chance to get really involved with Amnesty's work, and to feel as though I am doing something useful."

Local adoption groups work on all of Amnesty International's concerns. They maintain the same impartiality as the international movement—by being willing to work on any region and any political regime where human rights abuses occur.

When Amnesty International's delegation accepted the Nobel Peace Prize in 1977, they paid tribute to the people who were the driving force of the organization:

> "Let there be no mistake about who is being honored here today.... It is everyone who has ever written a letter asking for the release of a prisoner of conscience. It is everyone who has ever stood in a vigil mourning the death of a political prisoner. It is everyone who has ever handed out leaflets, stuffed envelopes, done the accounts. Human rights cannot be left to governments, legislators, and jurists. They are the concern and responsibility of the man and woman in the street, of the laborer, the office clerk, the student. Every name on every petition counts."

Student Groups

The enthusiasm and energy of young people surges through all of AIUSA's activities. Amnesty is committed to ensuring a better world for the next generation, and AIUSA tenaciously challenges young people to take responsibility for their future.

Groups of young activists committed to Amnesty International currently exist on over 2,700 high school, college, and university campuses across the United States. These organized groups, ranging from 15–100 in size, work on behalf of individual prisoners abroad, participate in country and issue campaigns, and organize events to expand human rights awareness.

The dramatic growth in Amnesty's student movement over the past years can be attributed partly to AIUSA's "Conspiracy of Hope" and the "Human Rights Now!" rock music concert tours. The number of student activists doubled then tripled following these 1986 and 1988 tours. The use of music and television has been a catalyst in raising the consciousness and voices of thousands of student activists in the US and abroad.

AIUSA has welcomed its new members by rapidly developing programs to bring students into the mainstream of international human rights work. *Student Action,* a monthly newsletter published by AIUSA, features articles on human rights issues and activities relating to the particular interest of student groups. Students also receive Urgent Actions two to four times a month which call for immediate response to the needs of prisoners around the world. Longer term campaign work is provided to the students via the "Action Pak" system. These Action Paks give detailed education, outreach, and action opportunities for the groups to work on during a 3–4 month period. Other forms of information and action are provided via special video and television projects, a 900-number action line, and internship opportunities with AIUSA.

Training and developing leadership skills is also a large part of the student program. Special student leadership trainings are organized annually by each of the five regions. Workshops on skills, countries, and issues are provided at regional conferences and the AIUSA Annual General Meeting. The ongoing Asylum Summer program brings 10–12 student activists to the Rio Grande Valley to volunteer in refugee relief organizations for 10 weeks each summer. This "hands-on" human rights work includes refugee issue trainings and leadership development. Other placement opportunities are being developed every year. The development of a nationalized leadership skills training program and a human rights speakers bureau for students are currently in the making for 1992.

Students show a unique ability to combine enjoyable group activities with serious and committed human rights work. They have taken leadership roles in numerous campaigns, pressing Burundi authorities to end political killings, protesting widespread "disappearances" in Peru, and building public pressure for a halt on use of the death penalty. They have used art poster contests, guerilla theater, music concerts, display tables, mock arrests, and issue forums; they have held rallies and lobbied public officials. These young people have created a national momentum, bringing human rights awareness and education to their campuses, communities, and into their own lives.

The nuts and bolts of group work

Some prisoners may only learn of a group's efforts on their behalf on release from prison, but their work can still be a source of inspiration.

> "I can't tell you how much I, and my wife too, appreciate your friendship and your concern about our sorrowful situation. . . ."
>
> *A released prisoner from Taiwan*

> "During these seven-and-a-half years of imprisonment, we were not aware that there were so many people all over the world concerned and fighting for our freedom. This knowledge is helping us now to face life again and to believe in this world and that evil can never win."
>
> *An ex-prisoner from Somalia*

In addition to their individual casework, groups also undertake long-term work focusing on AI issues, for example, the death penalty, the "disappeared," political killings, and country campaigns. Some groups work in networks focusing on certain countries and fighting other kinds of human rights violations—short-term detentions, mass arrests, "disappearances," political killings, torture, and other cruel and inhuman treatment. The details of cases can be disturbing. However, doing *something* which may help—such as a brief letter to the authorities—can be an antidote to the feelings of helplessness one may have upon hearing grim accounts of human rights violations.

Amnesty groups participate in shorter campaigns which highlight certain areas of human rights abuse that need concerted international pressure to bring about reform. Examples of such campaigns are the "Campaign Against Torture," the "Colombia, Stop the Death Squads" campaign, and the "Syria: Torture by the Security Forces" campaign. A group member explains, "Such campaigns give you a feel for another country and an insight into the life of people there. They give the group the opportunity to use imaginative campaigning techniques to capture the attention of the public." In the Colombia campaign, some groups held open evenings with Colombian food, music, dance, and even theater, during which supporters learned more about the country and had the opportunity to send appeals on behalf of victims of human rights violations there.

In a changing world, where ever more sophisticated methods of repression are being devised, group members fight back with new technology, sending telexes and faxes as well as the more traditional letters in response to Urgent Actions.

"His last words before he signed your release were, 'Not more bloody letters from Amnesty!' . . . !"
Colin Whittock

Letter writing is the basic technique used by groups. Letters are sent, where appropriate, to government authorities, heads of state, prison authorities, embassies, legal bodies, and sometimes (when to do so is possible and not dangerous to the recipients) to the prisoners themselves and their families. Group members receive advice on the types of letters to send, depending on the country concerned and the nature of the case. If a reply is received there are excited meetings as the group discusses how best to respond to the opening-up of a dialogue with a government minister, or even with the prisoner.

A conscientious objector to military service imprisoned in Greece (where there is no alternative service outside the military system and the length of imprisonment for a refusal to serve is punitive) wrote to one group:

> "I was glad to receive your letter which gave me courage to continue my struggle here in prison until my sentence is over.... Although you do not approve of compulsory military service for different reasons than I do [he is a Jehovah's Witness] you are to be praised for your point of view which defends human rights."

Often groups take on "investigation" cases, usually of prisoners whom Amnesty believes may be prisoners of conscience but does not have enough information to confirm that they have neither used nor advocated violence. In such instances the group tries to uncover more information by assiduous letter-writing to the authorities and other people likely to be able to provide information on the case. One group worked on the case of a prisoner in Africa for two years without even knowing where he was imprisoned, till one of their contacts in the United Kingdom was able to suggest where he was. The group was able to write to him there, and have now established an ongoing correspondence.

Campaign techniques include letter writing, circulating petitions, generating widespread publicity, holding public meetings, and urging professional associations and government representatives to intervene on behalf of prisoners.

Other work includes organizing vigils, circulating petitions, holding public meetings, putting on exhibitions, lobbying congress, embassies and professional associations, as well as generating local publicity for AI's campaigns and group activities.

In addition to keeping Amnesty International in the local media, groups spread the word about Amnesty and its work by speaking to other organizations: trade union locals, religious groups, women's groups, schools, colleges, and political groups. But publicity is also talking to friends, acquaintances and colleagues about Amnesty International—word of mouth is a powerful tool.

FUNDRAISING IS HUMAN RIGHTS WORK

Fundraising by groups is vital for AI to continue its work for victims of human rights abuses. Fundraising is therefore of extreme importance. It can also be fun, and for those with a creative impulse it can be quite rewarding. Groups find that fundraising combines the functions of bringing in much-needed cash *and* publicizing the work of Amnesty. One member organized an exhibit at a local shopping mall asking shoppers to sign and send greeting cards to prisoners of conscience, including Xu Wenli, imprisoned for 15 years in China for exercising his right to freedom of opinion and expression. She said, "We were astonished at the enthusiasm with which shoppers stopped to join in the signing on such a busy morning, and the generosity of their contributions . . . ."

AI groups sometimes raise money in varied and imaginative ways. One British group was able to present a check to Amnesty International when two of the members married and asked for their friends to donate money to Amnesty instead of spending it on wedding presents. Another enterprising young member took his pet cobra into school and allowed his schoolmates to stroke it for a fee!

AMNESTY'S NATURAL ALLIES: TARGET SECTORS

As Amnesty International developed as a movement, its first priority was naturally to build its own membership, structures, and working methods. It needed to establish its independence from particular governments, ideologies, or religions if it was to be effective in its task. Yet with the vastness of the problem which it had set itself to address, it also needed all the friends it could get.

AI recognized from its early days that there were other movements and organizations which would be natural allies in its work—and from which it drew many of its early members. The structures and working methods used for cooperating with such other organizations and movements are called "target sector work." Trade unions and religious organizations are among these "targets," from which AI wished to gain support. They were seen as natural allies, not only because they campaigned for particular social, economic, or religious rights, but because their existence would be threatened without the basic political freedoms which Amnesty's work helps to defend.

Trade unions, religious bodies, and educational, media, legal, medical, and women's organizations are all attacked at different times by governments who see their advocacy of specific rights or their general defense of human freedoms as a threat. In many cases these organizations have been banned and forcibly silenced, their property confiscated, or they have been infiltrated by or absorbed into the apparatus of the state. Individual leaders or members have been subjected to violations of their civil rights, imprisonment, torture, or execution.

Apart from the obvious shared concerns between AI and its "target sectors," there are many practical advantages to AI in working with them. AI's strength does not lie in armies deployed to defeat repressive governments, but in strength of political will and influence in the numbers of people prepared to stand up for human rights, and in their moral conviction. Organizations such as trade unions have considerable resources —human, political, financial, and technical. They can help communicate with and obtain the participation of large numbers of people in a wide range of occupations and professions.

If everyone supporting the aims of Amnesty International were to persuade the organizations to which they belonged to affiliate with AI, there would be the potential for a vast network of support. The full power and influence of the many social movements and organizations who stand for justice and truth, linked to the expertise and single-mindedness of AI, would be of incalculable value in the struggle for human freedom.

Chapter Twelve

AMNESTY'S VOLUNTEERS— WHAT YOU CAN DO

Few organizations can boast a work force with the expertise and commitment of AIUSA's Volunteer Leadership. For no pay and little thanks they work long hours advising and assisting the movement. They include the Country Coordination Groups, the Area Coordinators, the Student Area Coordinators, the Trainers, and the volunteer leaders of the Legal, Medical, and Educators Networks.

Country Coordination Groups

Country Coordination Groups (Co-Groups) focus on a particular country or region of the world. Members have expertise in that region and are the volunteer expert resources for AIUSA. They consult with staff on strategy. When a group is assigned the case of a prisoner from Manila, for example, the Philippines Coordination Group follows the group's progress and advises it on effective strategy for that particular region.

Area Coordinators

ACs help organize the activities of AIUSA groups and members in a particular state or area. With help from the regional office they arrange meetings, provide membership training, and assist groups in planning events, campaign work, and community organizing. ACs work closely with the groups in their areas,

"I'd like today's proceedings to take on an air of civilized justice—the Amnesty observer in in!" **Colin Whittock**

offering the kind of ongoing support that reflects a thorough familiarity with the character and activities of particular groups.

Student Area Coordinators

AIUSA's Student Area Coordinators perform a similar function to AIUSA's Area Coordinators, only they help AIUSA's burgeoning student membership.

Trainers

Trainers visit groups on request to lead workshops designed to help members increase the effectiveness of their human rights work. A group might, for example, arrange a training session to develop skills in fundraising, campaign strategizing, recruitment, or publicity. The death penalty coordinators from several groups in neighboring towns might ask for training on how to coordinate their international and United States death penalty work.

State and Regional Death Penalty Coordinators

State and Regional Death Penalty Coordinators are volunteer leaders who coordinate Amnesty International's work within a state or region to abolish the death penalty. In states which still have capital punishment, they play a key role in shaping the effort to limit or remove the death penalty in the state's legislature.

Legal Support Network

The Legal Support Network includes lawyers and other legal professionals who do legal research, and advise groups and staff on legal questions relating to Amnesty International's work. They might provide legal counsel or refer political asylum applicants to those who specialize in refugee or human rights laws.

Health Professionals Network

The Health Professionals Network performs a parallel role with doctors, nurses, and other health professionals who advise groups on the medical aspects of their prisoner work, and educate and involve medical associations and the public.

Human Rights Education Steering Committee

The Human Rights Education Steering Committee is made up of teachers of all levels, from early education to college and graduate school. Their goal is to help provide and introduce human rights education materials into school curriculum, and to coordinate educators who are active in Amnesty International.

WHAT YOU CAN DO

Amnesty International's strength lies in the convictions, work, and support of its groups and individuals. Those who join AI become a valuable part of a worldwide organization that works to protect human rights. As a member of an AI group you make a tremendous difference to the health, welfare, and even the life and death of people who truly need your help, people who are imprisoned, possibly being tortured, or maybe even facing execution.

Members of Amnesty come from all walks of life. They include social workers, lawyers, teachers, trade unionists, homemakers, students, journalists, doctors, nurses, retired people, artists, clergy, veterans, laborers, politicians, farmers.... The movement is open to anyone who supports its goals.

Starting a Group in Your Area

If there is no local Amnesty group in your area, you may wish to start one. The regional office will send you a packet of information on Amnesty's policies, structure, and group responsibilities. Tips on how to organize meetings, raise funds for your group and work with other AI groups, in addition to campaign strategy and letter writing, are also included.

If you decide to go ahead after reviewing these materials, the regional office will put you in touch with an Area Coordinator, an experienced volunteer leader in your area who can guide you further. They will also send you additional materials with which to interest others in helping to form the group. These materials will include more brochures, a recruitment video and flyer, a letter writing guide, an Amnesty International publications and a video catalog, a sample AI constitution, and a list of regional staff and volunteer leaders. A form for registering the group with the regional office once you have had a successful organizing meeting and have been approved for registration by the Area Coordinator will also be included.

As you and your group organize and sponsor special events, concerts, and seminars, distribute petitions and disseminate Amnesty International information, you will bring international abuses of human rights to public attention and rally support for human rights work.

Individual Members

There are many ways for people to become involved with Amnesty's work. Members actively contribute to the movement by paying dues ($25 a year for regular membership; $15 a year for students, senior citizens, and low income citizens) and writing letters. They can join Freedom Writers, the Urgent Action Network, or respond to appeals reported in *Amnesty Action,* a bimonthly newspaper which keeps them informed with news about Amnesty International and human rights worldwide. *Amnesty Action* allows members to participate in campaigns, anti-death penalty work, and individual prisoner cases.

Freedom Writers

Formed in 1986, Freedom Writers is a vast letter-writing source that can frequently generate a massive volume of mail on behalf of prisoners of conscience. Each Freedom Writer receives three cases per month from AIUSA, often cases already assigned to US adoption groups. So when needed, Amnesty International's Freedom Writers can create enormous pressure on a government to release a prisoner of conscience. In 1990, AIUSA Freedom Writers wrote thousands of letters on behalf of 36 men and women imprisoned around the world.

Urgent Action Network

Some call it Amnesty International's emergency room. In operation 24-hours a day, the Urgent Action Network is AIUSA's rapid response program. Amnesty realizes that the torture of detainees often occurs immediately upon arrest, and therefore it is necessary to respond quickly. Ten to fifteen thousand individuals agree to take action in cases of imminent torture or execution once, twice, four, or eight times a month.

Urgent Action (UA) appeals are sent by computer to the Urgent Action office in Nederland, Colorado from Amnesty's International Secretariat in London. Staff and volunteers at the Colorado office see that these UA appeals are mailed first class to network participants on the same day they are received at the office. UAs can also be posted in local papers or on computer bulletin boards. Participants write courteous letters to foreign government officials on behalf of victims. Telegrams, telexes, and faxes are employed as well. In some cases telephone calls to officials are requested.

Joan Baez

Participants in the Urgent Action Network may choose to write on behalf of colleagues or specifically where there is a legal or health concern. The Network maintains lists of health professionals, lawyers, political leaders, academics, unionists, journalists and writers, artists, and religious leaders who are committed to writing at least once a month on targeted cases. Language classes can be sent UA cases requesting letters in French or Spanish. Since 1978, the Urgent Action office has supplied individual women and women's groups with cases of women detainees whose basic human rights are being abridged. Individuals who wish to write appeals dealing with children as victims are sent one such case each month.

UA Network participants can also pledge the cost of monthly telegrams which are sent in their names within hours of receipt of the UA.

In 1989 the Urgent Action program handled 926 actions, 514 of which were first-issue Urgent Actions. Each UA case generated between 200 and 10,000 responses from letter-writers in the United States alone. There are Urgent Action Networks in 60 other member countries of Amnesty International. The number of letters written worldwide on most UA cases cannot be calculated with accuracy. Amnesty International believes there is improvement in the conditions of victims who are the focus of Urgent Action appeals.

HOW TO JOIN AMNESTY INTERNATIONAL

It's easy. Fill in the volunteer form at the back of this book and return it to AI, or call 1-800-55-AMNESTY. Your contribution, in whatever capacity you choose to become involved, will be deeply appreciated. There is no shortage of work to be done, and your membership will give you the unique satisfaction of being part of the most important movement of our time. There are many thousands of men, women, and even children who need our help. They call out to us silently from behind locked doors all over the world. We can set them free.

AIUSA OFFICES

National Office
Amnesty International USA
322 Eighth Avenue
New York, NY 10001
(212) 807-8400

Mid-Atlantic Regional Office
Amnesty International Mid-Atlantic
1118 22nd Street NW
Washington, DC 20037
(202) 775-5161

Northeast Regional Office
Amnesty International Northeast
58 Day Street, Davis Square
Somerville, MA 02144
(617) 623-0202

Southern Regional Office
Amnesty International South
740 West Peachtree
Atlanta, GA 30308
(404) 876-5661

Midwest Regional Office
Amnesty International Midwest
53 West Jackson, Rm. 1162
Chicago, IL 60604
(312) 427-2060

Western Regional Office
Amnesty International West L.A.
3407 West Sixth Street, Rm. 704
Los Angeles, CA 90020
(213) 388-1237

San Francisco Office
Amnesty International San Francisco
655 Sutter Street, Suite 402
San Francisco, CA 94102
(415) 441-3733

Urgent Action Network Office
AIUAN
P.O. Box 1270
Nederland, CO 80466
(303) 440-0913

Washington, DC Office
Amnesty International DC Office
304 Pennsylvania Ave. SE
Washington, DC 20003
(202) 544-0200

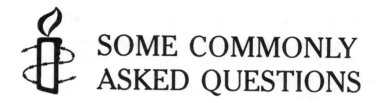

SOME COMMONLY ASKED QUESTIONS

What is a prisoner of conscience?

Prisoners of conscience are individuals who have been imprisoned solely because of their beliefs, sex, language, religion, or national origin, and who have not used or advocated violence. Amnesty calls on all governments to release them immediately and conditionally.

What is a political prisoner?

The term "prisoner of conscience" is narrowly defined; the term "political prisoner" is broader and applies to anyone whose imprisonment involves a political element. Amnesty International tries to ensure that *all* political prisoners are given a fair trial within a reasonable period of time.

What is a fair trial?

The United Nations sets out international standards for fair trials. Amnesty International urges all governments to follow these. Amnesty campaigns for fair and prompt trials for *all* political prisoners, whether or not they have advocated violence.

Is torture ever justified?

Torture is never acceptable under any circumstances, according to international law. Torturers may claim that torture produces confessions—and it does. Under torture, prisoners may confess to any allegation, even to crimes that they have not committed. Amnesty International opposes torture in all circumstances.

What is "cruel, inhuman, and degrading treatment"?

The term "cruel, inhuman, and degrading treatment" has not been defined by the U.N. General Assembly, but is intended to be interpreted so as to provide the widest possible protection against abuses, whether physical or mental. Such treatment may include, for example, prison conditions which do not allow prisoners to sit down, or keeping a prisoner blindfolded.

Amnesty International has found that the best way to stop cruel, inhuman, and degrading treatment is by using individual cases to illustrate what is wrong with the practice, and by asking or urging the government to stop that practice or change those conditions.

What are extra-judicial executions?

Extra-judicial executions are killings by the government or government-backed forces that are carried out outside the legal system. The term does not include killings by opposing factions during war.

Why does Amnesty International oppose the death penalty?

Amnesty International opposes the death penalty for several reasons: It is the ultimate cruel or degrading treatment a prisoner can receive; it does not deter crime; it is arbitrary and irrevocable; it is imposed unequally; and it is a gross violation of human rights.

What is an asylum seeker?

A person fleeing persecution in their own country will frequently seek asylum in another country. In these cases, national sections of Amnesty in that country will appeal to their own government to grant asylum and provide it with information about the human rights conditions from which the asylum seeker has fled.

Where does Amnesty International get its money?

Amnesty International relies entirely on donations from its members and the public. It must continue to be—and be seen to be—financially independent. The greatest part of the movement's funds come from small individual donations, the sections' membership fees, and local fund-raising drives. These make Amnesty a broad popular movement, backed by financial support from the public throughout the world.

Does Amnesty International use government money?

AI does not seek or receive any government money for its budget. It will accept contributions for humanitarian relief to prisoners, but only if AI administers the funds itself. It does not accept any donations that are directed for work on a specific country or case.

How does Amnesty International get its information?

AI uses a wide variety of sources, both public and private. The International Secretariat sends fact-finding missions to sensitive or troubled areas to assess the situation, interview prisoners, and meet with government officials. It also receives information from individuals and networks inside various countries. It subscribes to hundreds of newspapers and journals, and gets transcripts of radio broadcasts, government bulletins, reports from legal experts, and letters from prisoners and their families.

How does Amnesty International make sure it has the facts right?

All information that reaches the International Secretariat is carefully reviewed by the research staff. Details are cross-checked, every precaution is taken to avoid presenting an unconfirmed allegation as a fact. Before any statement is issued the text is reviewed at several different levels of the secretariat to make sure that it is accurate and falls within AI's mandate.

Isn't Amnesty International a political organization?

Amnesty is impartial—it does not support or oppose any government or political system. It believes human rights must be respected universally, and it takes up cases *whenever* it considers there are reliable grounds for concern, regardless of the ideology of the government or the beliefs of the victims.

Isn't Amnesty International interfering in the internal affairs of states?

Human rights transcend national boundaries. This principle has been recognized by the world's main intergovernmental organizations. The very fact that the United Nations has a Permanent Commission on Human Rights, which deals with human rights violations around the world, supports the view that the international community can and should keep a watch on the human rights practices of individual governments. Amnesty works on that principle, asking governments to conform to the human rights standards that they themselves have adopted internally and internationally.

Why does Amnesty International take up cases of people who have broken their country's laws?

National laws themselves often violate human rights standards. In many countries, emergency legislation drastically restricts the rights of all citizens, for example by allowing for lengthy detention without charge or trial. AI examines each situation, using a single, universal, internationally recognized standard of human rights. If a state is violating those rights, AI comes to the defense of the victims.

What countries does Amnesty International regard as the worst violators of human rights?

AI does not evaluate or rank governments according to their human rights records. For one thing, the repression practiced in various countries prevents the free flow of information about human rights abuses. Also, the techniques of repression and their impact vary widely. Instead of making comparisons, AI concentrates on trying to end the specific violations of human rights in each case.

Aren't human rights a luxury, especially in less developed countries?

There can be no double standard on human rights: they apply to everyone, everywhere. And economic, social, and cultural rights do not conflict with civil and political rights; both are essential in any society at all stages of development.

Does Amnesty International get results?

AI has heard from many prisoners, their families, and their lawyers who have thanked AI for its efforts on their behalf. Although it does not claim credit for the release of prisoners, many former prisoners have said that it was international pressure that secured their freedom or saved their lives, and the knowledge that AI was working on their cases that gave them hope.

Amnesty has helped to increase public awareness throughout the world about political imprisonment, torture, and the death penalty. This awareness has encouraged the news media to pay much more attention to human rights violations. AI has also helped to promote improved international standards for the protection of human rights. Bodies like the United Nations have taken important steps, such as declaring a universal ban on torture.

What do Amnesty International members do about human rights in their own country?

As an individual citizen or as a member of a civil liberties group, any member is free to become involved in domestic cases or causes. However, when working for AI, they must respect the principle of *international* protection of human rights. AI members and groups do not work on cases within their own countries or make statements about them. Under AI's rules, however, they may work for the abolition of the death penalty in their own country, press their own government to ratify international human rights treaties, try to ensure that refugees are not sent back to countries where they might face torture or execution or become prisoners of conscience, and play a part in local human rights education programs.

What is AI's policy on peace?

AI recognizes a link between peace and respect for human rights, but it works within a precise mandate and takes no position outside this mandate. AI does not, for example, take any position on various proposals for disarmament. Where issues related to peace and military conflict affect prisoners within AI's mandate, AI has developed policies, a number of which are discussed below.

Is it true Amnesty International has links with intelligence agencies?

No. AI is independent of all governments and government agencies. It acts openly and does not conduct espionage. No evidence has ever been produced to substantiate claims—made by governments of both the left and right—that AI is linked in any way to national intelligence services.

How do Amnesty International members participate in policy making?

AI is a participatory movement. Through their local *groups* and nationally based *sections,* members decide on the policy of the movement they finance. All national sections have their own internal structures for involving their members, and send representatives to the International Council Meeting where delegates from all over the world determine the movement's program.

What is AI's position on military, economic, and cultural relations?

AI does not take a stand on the legitimacy of military, economic, and cultural relations maintained with countries where human rights are violated, or on punitive measures such as sanctions or boycotts. AI does not address itself to the general economic or political system in any country, only to that country's observance of human rights within AI's mandate. Consequently, AI abstains from drawing conclusions of a political nature from its information.

What is AI's policy on military, security, and police transfers?

AI supports the introduction of legislation and regulations in all countries that supply military, security, and police equipment, requiring that transferring governments take into account the human rights situation in the receiving countries before making decisions about MSP transfers. AI is opposed to MSP transfers used for human rights violations within AI's mandate. AI may call for the termination of an MSP transfer if there is a direct—or indirect, but essential—link between the transfer and systematic widespread human rights violations. Any such call must be approved by Amnesty's International Executive Committee.

What is AI's position on violence?

AI takes no position on the question of violence. It does not identify with any of the parties to any conflict, nor does it presume to judge in any situation whether recourse to violence is justified or not. AI opposes torture and execution of all prisoners and advocates fair and prompt trials for all political prisoners, regardless of whether they are accused of using or advocating violence. However, AI seeks the immediate and unconditional release only of individuals imprisoned for the peaceful exercise of their human rights, whose imprisonment cannot be reasonably attributed to the use or advocacy of violence. AI is not bound to accept the assertion of a government, the interpretation of a court, or the claim of a prisoner as to whether an individual has used or advocated violence. The fact that a prisoner has been convicted of breaking the law or belongs to an organization whose aims call for the use of violence does not in itself preclude an individual from being a prisoner of conscience. AI evaluates and takes up each case on its own merits.

What is AI's policy on abuses by opposition groups?

AI condemns torture or execution of prisoners by anyone, including opposition groups. AI's mandate is based on international human rights standards which define the obligations of governments in protecting the rights of individuals. When governments curtail these rights, the organization urges them to take all necessary steps to restore them. When the offenses are committed by opposition groups, AI considers that it is within the jurisdiction of the government concerned to determine criminal responsibility and bring those responsible to justice. The exercise of this authority must conform to the government's commitments in international law.

Some opposition groups acquire a character and influence that makes them similar to governments. AI expects such groups to respect international human rights standards, and appeals to them to do so. An appeal from AI to such a group does not imply any legal or international status or recognition; it's only aim is to secure the protection of human rights that AI seeks to defend everywhere.

What is AI's policy on conscientious objection?

AI understands a conscientious objector to be a person who may be drafted for military service and who, for reasons of conscience or profound conviction arising from religious, ethical, moral, humanitarian, philosophical, political, or similar motives, refuses to perform armed service or participate directly or indirectly in wars or armed conflicts. AI considers such a person to be a prisoner of conscience if his or her imprisonment results from a number of related factors, such as inadequate provisions for conscientious objection or alternative service in the country's legal code.

A person who is not willing to state the reason for his or her refusal to perform military service is not adopted as a prisoner of conscience, unless it can be inferred from all the circumstances of the case that the refusal is based on conscientious objection. A person is not considered a prisoner of conscience if he or she is offered and refuses comparable alternative service outside the military.

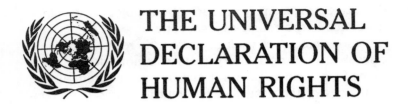

THE UNIVERSAL DECLARATION OF HUMAN RIGHTS

On December 10, 1948, the General Assembly of the United Nations adopted and proclaimed the Universal Declaration of Human Rights. Following this historic act, the Assembly called upon all Member countries to publicize the text of the Declaration and "to cause it to be disseminated, displayed, read and expounded principally in schools and other educational institutions, without distinction based on the political status of countries or territories."

PREAMBLE

Whereas recognition of the inherent dignity and of the equal and inalienable rights of all members of the human family is the foundation of freedom, justice and peace in the world,

Whereas disregard and contempt for human rights have resulted in barbarous acts which have outraged the conscience of mankind, and the advent of a world in which human beings shall enjoy freedom of speech and belief and freedom from fear and want has been proclaimed as the highest aspiration of the common people,

Whereas it is essential, if man is not to be compelled to have recourse, as a last resort, to rebellion against tyranny and oppression, that human rights should be protected by the rule of law,

Whereas it is essential to promote the development of friendly relations between nations,

Whereas the peoples of the United Nations have in the Charter reaffirmed their faith in fundamental human rights, in the dignity and worth of the human person and in the equal rights of men and women and have determined to promote social progress and better standards of life in larger freedom,

Whereas Member States have pledged themselves to achieve, in cooperation with the United Nations, the promotion of universal respect for and observance of human rights and fundamental freedoms,

Whereas a common understanding of these rights and freedoms is of the greatest importance for the full realization of this pledge,

Now, therefore, THE GENERAL ASSEMBLY *proclaims*

this

UNIVERSAL DECLARATION OF HUMAN RIGHTS

as a common standard of achievement for all peoples and all nations, to the end that every individual and every organ of society, keeping this Declaration constantly in mind, shall strive by teaching and education to promote respect for these rights and freedoms and by progressive measures, national and international, to secure their universal and effective recognition and observance, both among the peoples of Member States themselves and among the peoples of territories under their jurisdiction.

Article 1
All human beings are born free and equal in dignity and rights. They are endowed with reason and conscience and should act towards one another in a spirit of brotherhood.

Article 2
Everyone is entitled to all the rights and freedoms set forth in this Declaration, without distinction of any kind, such as race, color, sex, language, religion, political or other opinion, national or social origin, property, birth or other status.

Furthermore, no distinction shall be made on the basis of the political, jurisdictional or international status of the country or territory to which a person belongs, whether it be independent, trust, non-self-governing or under any other limitation of sovereignty.

Article 3
Everyone has the right to life, liberty and the security of person.

Article 4
No one shall be held in slavery or servitude; slavery and the slave trade shall be prohibited in all their forms.

Article 5
No one shall be subjected to torture or to cruel, inhuman or degrading treatment or punishment.

Article 6
Everyone has the right to recognition everywhere as a person before the law.

Article 7

All are equal before the law and are entitled without any discrimination to equal protection of the law. All are entitled to equal protection against any discrimination in violation of this Declaration and against any incitement to such discrimination.

Article 8

Everyone has the right to an effective remedy by the competent national tribunals, for acts violating the fundamental rights granted him by the constitution or by law.

Article 9

No one shall be subjected to arbitrary arrest, detention or exile.

Article 10

Everyone is entitled in full equality to a fair and public hearing by an independent and impartial tribunal, in the determination of his rights and obligations and of any criminal charge against him.

Article 11

1. Everyone charged with a penal offense has the right to be presumed innocent until proved guilty according to law in a public trial at which he has had all the guarantees necessary for his defense.

2. No one shall be held guilty of any penal offense on account of any act or omission which did not constitute a penal offense, under national or international law, at the time when it was committed. Nor shall a heavier penalty be imposed than the one that was applicable at the time the penal offense was committed.

Article 12

No one shall be subjected to arbitrary interference with his privacy, family, home or correspondence, nor to attacks upon his honor and reputation. Everyone has the right to the protection of the law against such interference or attacks.

Article 13

1. Everyone has the right to freedom of movement and residence within the borders of each State.

2. Everyone has the right to leave any country, including his own, and to return to his country.

Article 14

1. Everyone has the right to seek and to enjoy in other countries asylum from persecution.

2. This right may not be invoked in the case of prosecutions genuinely arising from non-political crimes or from acts contrary to the purposes and principles of the United Nations.

Article 15

1. Everyone has the right to a nationality.

2. No one shall be arbitrarily deprived of his nationality nor denied the right to change his nationality.

Article 16

1. Men and women of full age, without any limitation due to race, nationality or religion, have the right to marry and to found a family. They are entitled to equal rights as to marriage, during marriage and at its dissolution.

2. Marriage shall be entered into only with the free and full consent of the intending spouses.

3. The family is the natural and fundamental group unit of society and is entitled to protection by society and the State.

Article 17

1. Everyone has the right to own property alone as well as in association with others.

2. Not one shall be arbitrarily deprived of his property.

Article 18

Everyone has the right to freedom of thought, conscience and religion; this right includes freedom to change his religion or belief, and freedom, either alone or in community with others and in public or private, to manifest his religion or belief in teaching, practice, worship and observance.

Article 19

Everyone has the right to freedom of opinion and expression; this right includes freedom to hold opinions without interference and to seek, receive and impart information and ideas through any media and regardless of frontiers.

Article 20

1. Everyone has the right to freedom of peaceful assembly and association.

2. No one may be compelled to belong to an association.

Article 21

1.   Everyone has the right to take part in the government of his country, directly or through freely chosen representatives.

2.   Everyone has the right of equal access to public service in his country.

3.   The will of the people shall be the basis of the authority of government; this will shall be expressed in periodic and genuine elections which shall be by universal and equal suffrage and shall be held by secret vote or by equivalent free voting procedures.

Article 22

Everyone, as a member of society, has the right to social security and is entitled to realization, through national effort and international cooperation and in accordance with the organization and resources of each State, of the economic, social and cultural rights indispensable for his dignity and the free development of his personality.

Article 23

1.   Everyone has the right to work, to free choice of employment, to just and favorable conditions of work and to protection against unemployment.

2.   Everyone, without any discrimination, has the right to equal pay for equal work.

3.   Everyone who works has the right to just and favorable remuneration ensuring for himself and his family an existence worthy of human dignity, and supplemented, if necessary, by other means of social protection.

4.   Everyone has the right to form and to join trade unions for the protection of his interests.

Article 24

Everyone has the right to rest and leisure, including reasonable limitation of working hours and periodic holidays with pay.

Article 25

1.   Everyone has the right to a standard of living adequate for the health and well-being of himself and of his family, including food, clothing, housing and medical care and necessary social services, and the right to security in the event of unemployment, sickness, disability, widowhood, old age or other lack of livelihood in circumstances beyond his control.

2.   Motherhood and childhood are entitled to special care and assistance. All children, whether born in or out of wedlock, shall enjoy the same social protection.

Article 26

1.   Everyone has the right to education. Education shall be free, at least in the elementary and fundamental stages. Elementary education shall be compulsory. Technical and professional education shall be made generally available and higher education shall be equally accessible to all on the basis of merit.

2.   Education shall be directed to the full development of the human personality and to the strengthening of respect for human rights and fundamental freedoms. It shall promote understanding, tolerance and friendship among all nations, racial or religious groups, and shall further the activities of the United Nations for the maintenance of peace.

3.   Parents have a prior right to choose the kind of education that shall be given to their children.

Article 27

1.   Everyone has the right freely to participate in the cultural life of the community, to enjoy the arts and to share in scientific advancement and its benefits.

2   Everyone has the right to the protection of the moral and material interests resulting from any scientific, literary or artistic production of which he is the author.

Article 28

Everyone is entitled to a social and international order in which the rights and freedoms set forth in this Declaration can be fully realized.

Article 29

1.   Everyone has duties to the community in which alone the free and full development of his personality is possible.

2.   In the exercise of his rights and freedoms, everyone shall be subject only to such limitations as are determined by law solely for the purpose of securing due recognition and respect for the rights and freedoms of others and of meeting the just requirements of morality, public order and the general welfare in a democratic society.

3. These rights and freedoms may in no case be exercised contrary to the purposes and principles of the United Nations.

Article 30
Nothing in this Declaration may be interpreted as implying for any State, group or person any right to engage in any activity or to perform any act aimed at the destruction of any of the rights and freedoms set forth herein.

THE STATUTE OF AMNESTY INTERNATIONAL Articles 1 and 2

As amended by the 18th International Council, meeting in Aguas de Lindóla, Brazil, November 30–December 6, 1987

OBJECT

1. Considering that every person has the right freely to hold and to express his or her convictions and the obligation to extend a like freedom to others, the object of Amnesty International shall be to secure throughout the world the observance of the provisions of the Universal Declaration of Human Rights, by:

    a. irrespective of political considerations working towards the release of and providing assistance to persons who in violation of the aforesaid provisions are imprisoned, detained or otherwise physically restricted by reason of their political, religious or other conscientiously held beliefs or by reason of their ethnic origin, sex, color or language, provided that they have not used or advocated violence (hereinafter referred to as "prisoners of conscience");

    b. opposing by all appropriate means the detention of any prisoners of conscience or any political prisoners without trial within a reasonable time or any trial procedures relating to such prisoners that do not conform to internationally recognized norms;

    c. opposing by all appropriate means the imposition and infliction of death penalties and torture or other cruel, inhuman or degrading treatment or punishment of prisoners or other detained or restricted persons whether or not they have used or advocated violence.

METHODS

2. In order to achieve the aforesaid object, Amnesty International shall:

    a. at all times maintain an overall balance between its activities in relation to countries adhering to the different world political ideologies and groups;

    b. promote as appears appropriate the adoption of constitutions, conventions, treaties and other measures which guarantee the rights contained in the provisions referred to in Article 1 hereof;

    c. support and publicize the activities of and cooperate with international organizations and agencies which work for the implementation of the aforesaid provisions;

    d. take all necessary steps to establish an effective organization of sections, affiliated groups and individual members;

    e. secure the adoption by groups of members or supporters of individual prisoners of conscience or entrust to such groups other tasks in support of the object set out in Article 1;

    f. provide financial and other relief to prisoners of conscience and their dependents and to persons who have lately been prisoners of conscience or who might reasonably be expected to be prisoners of conscience or to become prisoners of conscience if convicted or if they were to return to their own countries, to the dependents of such persons and to victims of torture in need of medical care as a direct result thereof;

    g. work for the improvement of conditions for prisoners of conscience and political prisoners;

    h. provide legal aid, where necessary and possible, to prisoners of conscience and to persons who might reasonably be expected to be prisoners of conscience or to become prisoners of conscience if convicted or if they were to return to their own countries, and, where desirable, send observers to attend the trials of such persons;

    i. publicize the cases of prisoners of conscience or persons who have otherwise been subjected to disabilities in violation of the aforesaid provisions;

j. investigate and publicize the disappearance of persons where there is reason to believe that they may be victims of violations of the rights set out in Article 1 hereof;

k. oppose the sending of persons from one country to another where they can reasonably be expected to become prisoners of conscience or to face torture or the death penalty;

l. send investigators, where appropriate, to investigate allegations that the rights of individuals under the aforesaid provisions have been violated or threatened;

m. make representations to international organizations and to governments whenever it appears that an individual is a prisoner of conscience or has otherwise been subjected to disabilities in violation of the aforesaid provisions;

n. promote and support the granting of general amnesties of which the beneficiaries will include prisoners of conscience;

o. adopt any other appropriate methods for the securing of its object.

The full text of the Statute of Amnesty International is available from: Amnesty International USA, 322 Eighth Avenue, New York, NY 10001, Attn: Publications.

Index

YOU CAN HELP

Amnesty International Works impartially to free prisoners of conscience (men, women, and children imprisoned solely for their beliefs, race, or ethnic origin who have neither used nor advocated violence), for fair and prompt trials for all political prisoners, and to abolish torture and executions.

I would like to join Amnesty International USA. Enclosed are my dues:

☐ Individual $25

☐ Student / Senior Citizen / Limited Income $15

☐ I understand that Amnesty International depends upon the generosity of its members. Therefore, I would like to make an additional contribution. For membership dues and donation I enclose a check for:

_____$50 _____$75 _____$100 _____$250 _____other

Contributions to Amnesty International USA are tax deductible.

I would like to participate in Amnesty International's work. Please send me more information about (check as many as applicable):

☐ Local Groups ☐ Health Professionals
☐ Campus Groups ☐ Legal Professionals
☐ Urgent Action Network ☐ Educators Network
☐ Freedom Writers Network ☐ Individual Letter Writing

Name _____

Address _____

City _____

State _____ Zip _____

AHB91

Bulk copies of this book
are available at special discounts
to groups and organizations.

For further details contact:

Hunter House Inc., Publishers
PO Box 847
Claremont CA 91711
Phone (714) 624-2277
Fax (714) 624-9028

Hunter House also publishes books in

- ❑ current affairs & social issues

- ❑ family & self-help

- ❑ psychology & psychotherapy

- ❑ health & nutrition

- ❑ mysticism & New Age

- ❑ fiction & writing

To receive a copy of our catalog, please mark categories you are most interested in, fill in the form below and mail to:

Hunter House Inc., Publishers, PO Box 847, Claremont CA 91711

Name _____

Address _____

_____

City/State Zip _____

Phone _____